BEHIND THE POWER

The Compelling Influence of a Praying Wife

Dr. Wanda A. Turner

Treasure House

An Imprint of
Destiny Image® Publishers, Inc.
P.O. Box 310
Shippensburg, PA 17257-0310

"For where your treasure is, there will your heart be also."
Matthew 6:21

ISBN 0-7684-3032-1
Library of Congress Catalog Card Number 2001 132710

For Worldwide Distribution
Printed in the U.S.A.

This book and all other Destiny Image, Revival Press,
MercyPlace, Fresh Bread, Destiny Image Fiction,
and Treasure House books are available
at Christian bookstores and distributors worldwide.

For a U.S. bookstore nearest you, call **1-800-722-6774**.
For more information on foreign distributors,
call **717-532-3040**.
Or reach us on the Internet: **www.destinyimage.com**

Dedication

*To my mother, Mary M. Stallworth,
and my "other mother," Hattie Mae Davis,
affectionately called "Mama Mae."*

*Special love and regards to Lewis Jr.,
my oldest brother. Thanks for placing
a love for words in my heart, and more
so thanks for teaching me to read
when I was three years old.*

Acknowledgments

*God's scribe, Michelle Jones,
and all "Calling First Ladies, Inc.,"
who inspired this project.*

Endorsements

The issue of power has been the subject of thousands of years of study, review, and investigation. The nature of power is as complex as any attempt to define it, yet the pursuit of power is inherent and basic to human nature.

The Bible's use of the word *dominion* in the Creation account (see Gen. 1:26,28) implies that God's purpose in creating man was to exercise a measure of delegated power and authority over the earth. Both the man and the woman received the power of dominion; however, the genders exercise this power differently. While man's power is released through his position, woman's power seems to be released through her influence. Women have a tremendous responsibility to manage and regulate this power and its positive or negative influence on men.

In *Behind the Power*, Dr. Wanda Turner has captured the awesome responsibility inherent in the exercise of the God-given power each human possesses. Her focus on the female factor provides unique insights for both women and men, and helps us understand the use and abuse of power. This book is a must-read for all who desire a fresh perspective on an age-old dilemma.

Dr. Myles Munroe
Bahamas Faith Ministries International

If you are a woman who is earnestly seeking direction in your walk on this road of life...look no farther! Dr. Wanda Turner has written a book that will give you exactly what you need and probably more than what you asked for! Incorporating the Word of God along with humor, common sense, and a wisdom that only comes from experience, Dr. Turner redefines what power really is and where it really comes from. Most importantly, she outlines how every woman of God can receive it! All I can say is "Hallelujah!"

Natalie Cole
Entertainer, Author

Anyone can have power if they want it. Most *think* they have it, but many don't yet realize that *true* power is one of a different nature, and the way to get it is really simple. First, we need to know what true power is and then follow God's order to maintain it and actually use it in our lives. It comes in many forms, shapes and sizes in this world, but the kind of power that lasts is only found in God.

In this book, Dr. Turner explicitly and powerfully explains what power is, how to get it and how to keep it. If you are ready to walk in a "new" you, endued with true power, then read on. Although it is geared toward women, the knowledge in this book about power will edify the spirit, mind and soul of anyone.

Bishop Eddie L. Long, D.D, D.H.L.
Senior Pastor
New Birth Missionary Baptist Church

Behind the Power is an autobiographical sketch that is inclusive of all women. You may be single, a mother, single mother, woman in ministry, executive, prostitute, virgin, politician, or wife of a famous athlete/businessman—it doesn't matter. This book challenges women to embrace their uniqueness and become empowered through a relationship with the Power behind the power. This book will cause women to realize their divine destiny and become women of power.

Cookie Johnson
Wife of Magic Johnson
Magic Johnson Foundation

Behind the Power is a thought-provoking, insightful, God-inspired book from a daughter of God, a wife to the Son, and a vessel of honor. As you read it, you will grow and understand that true power comes from our source, God, and that we are most powerful when we walk according to His will.

This book is a much-needed tool to balance us in a society where power is misperceived as money, sex, and titles. It gets us back on track.

Judge Mablean Ephriam
Divorce Court, TV series

For those women who either are married to a man of power or are in the seat of power themselves, this book will serve as a useful and valuable tool. Insights into the various aspects of power-influenced relationships are plentiful in this latest work by one of God's most gifted servants.

Mrs. Serita A. Jakes
First Lady
The Potter's House
Dallas, TX

Contents

Everybody notices him. Even those who pretend not to notice give themselves away. Conversations fall off of mid-thought cliffs. Women fidget and smile more. Men stand a little taller. Some shoot invidious sidelong glances when they know he's not looking. But I'm looking. I watch them all...admiring, following, serving, grinning, seeking, adoring, hoping.

He is a man of power. But more importantly he is my husband. That hand that shakes so many other hands holds my heart. Those ears that receive much praise also receive my comfort, encouragement and counsel. His confidence is nurtured in my arms. He is covered by my prayers. As he allows God to take him, break him, bless him and feed him to the world, I myself am broken and used of God to restore, replenish and renew him.

I marvel sometimes at how much they expect from him. I marvel more at how seldom it occurs to them what they inadvertently expect from me. When they have picked his mind clean of wit and wisdom, I am left with the bones of his focus and attention. When they have wrung from him every smile and hello, I am left with his dry expression. When they have gotten the peak of his performance, when they have ignored the clock and his slowing step to heap on his slumping shoulders the burden of their endless questions, concerns and criticisms, I am left to watch him sleep on his day off.

How do I pour into his life without feeling so empty? How do I support him without feeling abandoned? How do I stand behind his power without resenting it?

"A Woman Behind the Power"

Fear not; for thou shalt not be ashamed: neither be thou confounded; for thou shalt not be put to shame....For thy Maker is thine husband; the Lord of hosts is His name...

And I will betroth thee unto Me for ever; yea, I will betroth thee unto Me in righteousness, and in judgment, and in lovingkindness, and in mercies.

I will instruct thee and teach thee in the way which thou shalt go: I will guide thee with Mine eye.

"The Power"

Chapter One

Real Power

Who are you?

"...God said, It is not good that the man should be alone; I will make him an help meet for him" (Gen. 2:18). You are the solution to the first problem in the universe. You are the first hero—or *shero*—sent to rescue man from his incompleteness. Magnificent was your creation; it was like nothing else in heaven or on earth. You are the only thing made whose need was declared by God *before* you were formed.

So important is that distinction that God wouldn't even give Eve to Adam until he understood his need for her. He waited until Adam had named every beast and bird and then saw that he was alone. Scripture says "there was not found an help meet for him" (Gen. 2:20b). Imagine Adam, at first excited as each set of animals is brought before him: ram and ewe, cow and bull, peacock and peahen. But as the last two creatures male and female received their names and scurried, galloped or flew off, it became clear that something was dreadfully wrong. Where was his? His...what? He desired her and yet could not say so, because she did not exist.

So God caused Adam to sleep, and when he woke up, God brought him Eve. And like God, in whose image he was made, Adam declared his need for Eve before he named her. "This is now bone of my bones, and flesh of my flesh: she shall be called Woman..." (Gen. 2:23).

Quite a few years later, you were among the 120 who waited in the Upper Room. Jesus had just boarded a cloud bound for Heaven. All of you watched Him go, then watched the sky when you couldn't see Him anymore. But His promise rang in every ear and lingered in every heart: "But ye shall receive power, after that the Holy Ghost is come upon you: and ye shall be witnesses unto me both in Jerusalem, and in all Judaea, and in Samaria, and unto the uttermost part of the earth" (Acts 1:8). So you waited...and you did indeed receive power.

The question is, what do you plan to do with it?

Your Divine Destiny

When the Holy Ghost fell at Pentecost, He fell on you, woman of God. Your sisters in Christ prayed, praised and pressed their way through to Him along with Peter, James, John and the rest. The prophet Joel didn't leave you out when he said, "And it shall come to pass in the last days, saith God, I will pour out of My Spirit upon all flesh" (Acts 2:17a). "All flesh" includes your flesh. You were among the servants of God who would prophesy, dream and see signs and wonders.

Woman is as much a part of the Master's plan and purpose as man. Why then are we so reluctant to claim our God-given power? When did power become such a "masculine" concept? Where does the Scripture say that the woman, who is to be treated as the "weaker vessel," possesses a weaker spirit?

Within these pages, you will meet some very powerful women. They are married, single, divorced, mothers, daughters, sisters, leaders, widows, beautiful, bruised, broken, victorious, mistake-making, moving, shaking, green, grown, lonely, laughing, striving, surviving, *powerful* women. And in case you haven't guessed yet, you are among them. Your divine destiny is to be a woman of power. You are powerful, woman of God, not because you are married to a man of power—though some of you are married to great men. It is not because you have power on your job or in your home either, though some of you do carry such authority. It isn't even because you sing, pray, preach or teach powerfully at your church. No, precious sister, your steps were sovereignly ordered to bring you into a life of infinite power because *you belong to God*. He made you so that He could dwell in you in the fullness of His glory.

You are called, appointed and anointed to be a "woman behind the power," that power being the unlimited, unshakable, unstoppable, unbreakable Spirit of your Father in Heaven. When God stepped out on nothing and declared it something, then spoke something into *some things*, that was power. When dark became light, light became color, and color became form, that was power. When quiet birthed sound, sound birthed song, and song praised Him, that was power. When He told the sea to back up because He wanted to see the land He'd made, that was power. And when He gathered up a handful of dust and made a man, then gathered up a handful of man and made a woman, that was power. But when He took some of His own power and sent His Son here to live, die and be resurrected, He made His power available for you.

It was always God's plan for you to have power. Genesis 1:28 says God blessed *them*—the man and the woman—and told *them* to be fruitful and multiply, and replenish the earth and subdue it. He told *them* to have dominion over every living thing that moved upon the earth. But somewhere between the Garden and the New Millennium, too many people got the idea—the wrong idea—that power was merely the ability or authority to control, command, conform or correct people or circumstances. Somewhere along the way, power stopped being about giving and started being about taking. Sin corrupted power, and dominion became domination; submission became subjugation; humility became shame; and expectation became entitlement.

Today, power is measured in visibility, accountability, viability and responsibility. Are you big? Are you bad? Are you rich? Are you the boss? If you can answer yes to one or all of the above, then according to the world, you have power. More accurately, you have *the world's* power. Granted, that can get you pretty far. Just ask the Ted Turners, Bill Gateses and Oprahs of this world. Ask the athletes, actors and actresses who step ahead of you at those exclusive restaurants. The world's power does have its privileges but it also has its problems. Ask the politicians who cut the funding for the after-school program at your child's school. Ask the boss's unqualified nephew who just got promoted over you. Ask that drug dealer's mother who's looking the other way so the rent will get paid.

But you're not called to desire, pursue or demand the world's power. Your goal—and the goal of this book—is to unveil, understand and then unleash God's power in your life. The power you're heir to is not simply the power to subdue or dominate; it is the power to become a new creature and inspire that same desire in others. It is the power to overcome the pain and bitterness of your past. The power you have access to is the power to change the way you see the world and the way the world sees you. It is the power to be whole, to stand and to grow. This power doesn't grow or diminish with your bank balance or fade with age. It doesn't disappear if you get laid off or when your children act up. This is *real* power—and it's yours for the asking.

Defining Power

Here would be a good place to establish a clear, working definition of power. One of the earmarks of satan's handiwork is when things that were once so simple become complicated and unnecessarily complex. The concept of power is no different. Think about it. In the world, power could be money, unless you have something the world wants, like a new technology. Then knowledge is power. Of course, if you don't know the right people, or if those people don't like you, then your knowledge isn't worth much. On the other hand, you could be poor, stupid and 7'10" tall. If you play even mediocre basketball, somebody's going to throw a lot of money at you and *presto!* You've got power. Of course, that could all go away if you fall down and break your leg.

Then there are those who are powerful because other people want to watch them in movies or on television or see them in music videos. If you don't think they're powerful, ask a few teenagers to tell you who they'd rather be when they grow up, the President or Puff Daddy. Experience used to count for something. Now youthfulness carries more clout, so seasoned, intelligent executives are forced into early retirement so that empty-headed hotshots can take over.

Worldly power is a confusing concept at times. That makes sense; after all, satan is the author of confusion. One of the beautiful things about God is His simplicity. His goal is to enlighten us, not confuse us. Thus He always gives us order, then gives us the option to follow it or reject it. This truth is obvious when it comes to power.

Throughout Scripture, when God exercises His power, it is for one of three reasons: to show Himself *to* His people, to show Himself *for* His people, or to show Himself *in* His people. He shows Himself to us to guide, encourage, comfort and enable us. He shows Himself for us to protect, vindicate and validate us. He shows Himself in us so others can see Him. Whatever the reason, when God shows up, power shows up. When He doesn't show up, neither does power. With this in mind, we can be said to have real power simply when God shows up. Look then at the following definition:

Power is the ability and authority to recognize or reveal God.

Both ability and authority are necessary to access and exercise God's power. It's not enough to have ability if God hasn't given you permission to use it. Samson learned that the hard way. After Delilah cut his hair and the Philistines came to seize him, the Word says Samson "awoke out of his sleep, and said, I will go out as at other times before, and shake myself. And he [knew] not that the Lord was departed from him" (Judg. 16:20b).

You also can have authority but no ability. We read in Mark 6:7 that Jesus began to send the disciples out to minister, giving them "power over unclean spirits." Why then were they unable to cast an unclean spirit from a young boy in Mark 9? Jesus said, "This kind can come forth by nothing, but by prayer and fasting." The disciples had been given the authority, but they lacked ability because they had not given themselves totally to God through prayer or totally denied themselves through fasting. Sometimes God wants our total attention and devotion before He releases His power.

At times our unbelief will short-circuit our ability. The children of Israel were not allowed to enter the Promised Land because of their unbelief. Disobedience is another way to curtail

God's power. Saul lost his kingdom through disobedience. The Lord took His Spirit (power) from Saul and gave it to David.

God can be recognized by us or revealed through us. When He is recognized by us, our power changes us. It makes it possible to stand in a trial, have peace in a storm or hear the voice of God when everything you see conspires to discourage and depress you. This power is knowledge, understanding, wisdom and the fear of the Lord. When we operate with it, we find joy unspeakable and the ability to love, forgive and help others.

When God is revealed through us, our power changes others. God revealed is always an outpouring of our ability to recognize Him. He can't be seen *through* us if He is not first seen *by* us. When people see you praising God with your broken heart, your pile of bills and your crazy kids, it makes a powerful statement. It says He's still on the throne and you still trust Him to move on your behalf. It says if you can handle it, maybe somebody else can handle it too. When others see God restore, replace and renew the desolate places in your life, it can inspire them to know the same God you know.

Power is the ability and authority to recognize or reveal God, but how do we make it ours? And how do we know when it is ours? Well, look at God. He manifests Himself to us as Father, Son, and Holy Spirit. That said, real power is the ability and authority to recognize or reveal the Father, the Son, and the Holy Spirit. God is seen in terms of His relationship with us. Therefore, a "woman behind the power" is one who is:

A *Daughter* of the Father
A *Wife* of the Son
A *Vessel* of the Holy Spirit

As the daughter of the Father, you are covered by power. The woman who is a wife to the Son is attached to power. The vessel of the Holy Spirit is filled with, energized by and guided by power. A woman behind the power, be she single, married, working or not, mother to many or just one, or even none, needs to be these three things before she can effectively be anything else. Let's take a look at them individually.

Daughter

"Our Father which art in heaven..." Dana had read these words and said them many times. But one day, in her prayers, she realized that she didn't really see God as her "father." In fact, she wasn't sure what that meant. "Show me Yourself as 'father,'" she prayed that same day. She didn't know what she was asking for. There was no picture of it in her mind, so there was no expectation beyond that God would grant her request.

Her biological father had abandoned the family when she was just ten. Now in her thirties, Dana was just then making the connection between his absence and her inability to see God as her Father or herself as His daughter. "I didn't know what was missing, because...it was *missing*. I didn't know what I didn't have because I never had it. But if God was calling Himself that in the Bible, I thought, 'I want to know what it is, and I want it, *whatever* it is.'"

Not long after she prayed that prayer, Dana had a conversation with a pastor friend of hers. Somehow they started talking about her childhood. He asked her if there was ever a time that she would have wanted God to be there when He wasn't. Suddenly, a particularly painful memory surfaced. An eight-year-old Dana had gone to her father to ask for help with her math homework. Her father was impatient with her and told her that she was stupid if she didn't understand what seemed perfectly simple. "I'm not stupid!" she remembers exploding. "This is fifth-grade math, and I'm in the third grade! *This is supposed to be hard!*" She never asked for help again...from anyone. She went through junior high, high school and college without asking for help. If she didn't understand something in Chapter Six, she'd go all the way back to Chapter One and struggle until the answer presented itself.

"Where would you have wanted God to be when that happened?" her friend asked. "I would have wanted Him to be right in the middle of us. I'd have wanted Him to catch every mean thing my dad said to me before it got to me. Then I'd have wanted Him to turn around and face me and tell me all the things a father is supposed to tell his daughter." God chose that moment to speak to Dana. *That's exactly where I was. If I had not been there, you would have believed what he told you. And if I hadn't turned around and faced you and told you what to say to him, you would not have had an answer for him.*

So many children grow up believing the negative things their parents tell them. But God had been there to protect Dana, the way a father protects his daughter. He had always been there. He loved her with a father's love, telling her—as she was telling her earthly father—that she was intelligent, strong and special (just like her real heavenly Daddy). To know God as Father is to know His protection. It also means knowing that you are the apple of His eye, a treasure He jealously possesses.

Becoming a daughter of God is accomplished simply by seeking to know Him as your Father. God says to us through His prophet Jeremiah that "ye [shall] call upon Me, and ye shall go and pray unto Me, and I will hearken unto you. And ye shall seek Me, and find Me, when ye shall search for Me with all your heart. And I will be found of you..." (Jer. 29:12-14). His arms are big enough to hug you, if you'll enter His embrace. His lap is big enough to hold you, if you care to crawl up into it. His sleeve will catch every tear, if you want to cry. He will protect you. He *wants* to protect you. Jesus said no one would pluck you from the Father's hand.

Many of you have settled for less in your lives because you have not known the power that comes from understanding just what your Father says about you. "Fear not: for I have redeemed thee, I have called thee by thy name; thou art Mine" (Is. 43:1b). "I will never leave thee, nor forsake thee" (Heb. 13:5b). "Many daughters have done virtuously, but thou excellest them all" (Prov. 31:29). When was the last time you asked God to tell you what He thinks of you, how He feels about you, what He desires for you and from you? Oh, how precious also are His thoughts unto you! How great is the sum of them! (See Psalm 139:17.)

A daughter depends on her father for provision. Deuteronomy 8 says God gives us power to get wealth. Scripture is, among other things, a testimony of God's desire and ability to provide His children with everything they need and more. Peter says God's power has given us everything we need for life and godliness (see 2 Pet. 1:3).

Daughters seek their fathers' approval, attention and acceptance. God expects us to seek those things from Him—and He is ready to give them. There is nothing more brilliant than the smile of a daughter who knows her father's favor. That daughter knows she is valued. That daughter doesn't seek validation of the fact that she matters to somebody. She graciously *accepts confirmation* that it is already so.

A woman who knows her Father will not let some fool take advantage of her, mistreat her or demean her. She will not walk with her chin on her chest. God's daughters—those who walk in the truth of that relationship—don't accept satan's lies at face value. You are fearfully and wonderfully made. Shame is not your inheritance. You will be free from the pain of your past. There is life after a dead marriage. There is no mistake so big that it can't be used to bless you and bless others. That brother is not your last chance at love. That husband does love you, even though he's choosing to distance himself from you right now. He will cherish you again. You just have to be plugged into your Power Source. Your Daddy is waiting for you to run to Him so He can show you just how much He wants to do for you.

Wife

Ray laughs as he talks about a female friend of his. "When me and my boys talk about the kind of women we'd like to marry, her name comes up all the time. There's something about her. It's like there's something *on* her. So we know that if we're gonna step to her, we gotta step correct, or God might hurt us!"

Frank Wilson, husband of author P. Bunny Wilson, remembers his second date with Bunny, at her 50th birthday party. He says he was thinking less-than-holy thoughts about this woman he had just met when the Spirit of the Lord spoke up and said, "That's your wife." That slowed down his thoughts. But what stopped them was the next thing he heard. "That's your wife, but she's *My woman*." Frank said that was enough to completely correct his behavior toward the woman he would eventually marry.

Alisa remembers times in her marriage when stress, discontentment and unexpressed anger were taking their toll. Conversations with her husband were more like wrestling matches, each one trying to be heard, validated, appreciated and absolved while each one forgot to hear, validate, appreciate and absolve the other.

Alisa was struggling with some issues in her heart that made it difficult to give in. Finally, her husband stepped back. "He said the Lord told him, 'She's Mine. You can't grow, fix, heal or chastise that part of her. I'll take care of that. Let Me deal with her.' And He did."

They say behind every great man there is a great woman. Well, there is no man greater than Jesus and when we choose to be His bride on this earth, we become great by association. The woman who is the wife of the Son knows what it's like to be cherished. She knows tenderness, romance and passion. You don't believe it? Who do you think made the last sunset you saw and created the fragrance of every flower you love? Who gave His life for you? For *you*. Until you make His love for you personal, you won't be able to recognize His kiss in the morning or the bouquet of new mercies He left at the foot of your bed.

A woman who walks on the arm of the King of kings and Lord of lords is easily spotted. She's the single woman who isn't desperate to marry the first guy who buys her a burger and tells her she's pretty. She's the wife whose pleasure is serving her husband. She's that career woman who just closed that multimillion dollar deal, then got up to get her own coffee as well as some for her assistant. She's the single mother who hasn't seen a dime of child support and still lets her kids see their daddy. She's that virgin who's waiting for marriage. She's that minister who was not allowed behind the pulpit, so she preached the house down from beside it. She's a woman with a tumor, with less than a year to live, and who has joy unspeakable. She's walking praise and worship. She's "peace in spite of" and "faith in the midst of." She's a "kept woman"—kept safe in the secret place of the Almighty.

Becoming the wife of the Son is accomplished by simply saying yes to Him when He comes looking for you. "Behold, I stand at the door, and knock: if any man [or woman] hear My voice, and open the door, I will come in to him, and will sup with him, and he with Me" (Rev. 3:20). The more time we spend with Jesus, getting to know Him, trust Him and love Him, the more we begin to walk in the power associated with Him. He is the Word, and the woman who hides that Word in her heart has her path of life lit by the truth of it.

A wife knows her husband intimately. She knows his likes and his dislikes. She avoids those things that disappoint him and remembers those things that make him smile. Wives are visible representations of their husbands' position, ability, love and strength. The husband of the Proverbs 31 woman is praised in the gates because of what her behavior says about him. What do you say about your husband with your actions? Proverbs 12:4 says a virtuous woman is a crown to her husband. Are you a crown to yours? Is it a crown encrusted with the jewels of your wisdom, comfort, understanding, love, honesty, tenderness and generosity? Or is it a crown of thorns piercing his skin every time you open your mouth to slash him with your evil words? In the same way, what kind of wife have you been to Jesus? Do people know what kind of husband He is *by your actions*? When was the last time somebody praised Jesus because of what your behavior said about Him?

A good wife is committed to her husband. Are you committed to yours? Is there anything Jesus could ask of you that you would refuse Him? Would you stay on that job that works your nerves? Would you stop hollering at your kids? Would you break off that unsanctified relationship? Would you get up in the morning and pray? Would you praise Him? Would you spend some time with Him in the Word? Would you remember that He loves you more than anyone else in your life? Would you learn to trust Him?

The Kingdom of God is a community property kingdom. Once you marry the Son, what's yours is His and what's His is yours. When you think about all that you gave Jesus when you two got together, and all that He gave you in return, you ought to get on your knees and thank Him like you've got 10,000 tongues! You did give Him your "stuff," didn't you? You know, your sorrow, your issues, your anger, your guilt and your bitterness. If you haven't, He's waiting for it right now. He's waiting to take what you've got and give you joy, peace, wisdom, patience, love, forgiveness and so much more. Then you'll be free. All that junk that's been sapping your strength will be yours no more. And you can enjoy the power of an intimate relationship with the Lover of your soul and all the perks that come with that holy hookup.

Vessel

Her girlfriends don't know how she does it. Chris is a first-grade teacher and a student living in Los Angeles. She's working on a Master's degree and a teaching credential at the same time. She is a single mother with two children in a private Christian school. She owns her home and her car is paid for. She manages without any financial contribution from her children's father. Money usually runs out before the month does, but "ain't nobody starving and ain't nobody naked." She can't think about it for too long without crying. "I don't know how it happens. Sometimes I'm late paying the kids' tuition, but they just give me favor. If I add up the house note, school, food and bills, then look at what I make, it doesn't add up! I see people making twice what I do who can't make ends meet. I don't know why He loves me like this. I didn't do anything for it. I just do what I can, and He just takes care of me and my kids."

When we do what we can and let God take care of the rest, we are living filled with and fueled by the Holy Spirit. When we empty ourselves of ourselves and allow Him to indwell us, we find out what it means to be more than a conqueror. The Holy Spirit comforts, convicts and constrains us. He shows us the very hearts of people. He makes a way out of no way. He'll show you the stars in your darkest night. The Holy Spirit will take $10 and stretch it into a week of dinners for you and your children. He will find that offering in the bottom of your purse when you thought you didn't have a mite to give. He will find you in that emergency room and have a specialist "happen" by and look at your chart. He'll help you love those folks who hate you. He'll watch your husband get laid off and have him run out of gas right in front of a place that's hiring. He'll make you lose your keys at Wednesday evening Bible study so you can't creep over to your boyfriend's to spend the night. Then He'll put them next to some fine godly brother who will walk you to your car and ask you out for coffee.

Operating in the power of the Holy Spirit is accomplished when we yield to Him in every circumstance. When we allow Him to guide us, He makes our paths straight. When we allow Him to convict us of our sin, we are led to righteousness. When we allow Him to fight our battles for us, we cease striving and know God.

When we allow Him to keep us peaceful in our storms, we are changed from glory to glory. When we follow His lead, surrender to His gentle nudges, and respond humbly to whatever He shows us in our hearts, we have taken into ourselves the power to do all things, overcome all things and endure all things.

"But the Comforter, which is the Holy Ghost, whom the Father will send in My name, He shall teach you all things, and bring all things to your remembrance, whatsoever I have said unto you" (Jn. 14:26). He is sent by the Father in the name of the Son. To know His power is to know Theirs.

The most important thing to remember about a vessel is that it is always available. When was the last time you wanted to put flowers in a vase and the vase said no? Likewise, the Spirit expects to fill you and adorn the world with you—but at *His* discretion, which is according to God's will. Who are we to tell the One who made us how, when, or where we are to be used?

The Bible tells us that after Jesus was baptized He was led into the wilderness to be tempted by satan. Matthew says He was "led up of the Spirit." Mark's account says, "And immediately the Spirit driveth Him into the wilderness." And Luke describes our Lord as "being full of the Holy Ghost" and "led by" that Spirit into the wilderness. Jesus was led and pushed from the outside at the same time He was being led and pulled at from the inside. The three passages use similar but distinct ideas. The word *driveth* used in Mark is a picture of something being pulled up from where it is and cast forth or ejected. Luke presents the idea of one who is hurried or dragged by force. Matthew uses a Greek word that means to "sail away" or "launch forth." It is a navigational term. So Jesus, as a vessel of the Holy Spirit, was completely at the mercy of that same Spirit.

How many times have we felt helpless in our circumstances? We watched that relationship fall apart or that job "eject" us into the unemployment line. We have suffered through the illness or death of a loved one, confused. Why would a God who says He loves us allow such a thing to happen?

Imagine for a minute what it must feel like to be a baby in your mother's womb. You have everything you need: food, water, warmth, comfort, security. It doesn't get any better than that.

Then, one day, the walls around you begin to move...gently at first. Then the movement becomes violent, seemingly unaware of your existence, much less your comfort. If you knew what was really going on, would you handle the upheaval better? Birth is one of the most violent things that can happen to a human being. But it is so vital to the survival of the child that God does not leave the timing of it or the process of it up to the child, or his or her mother, for that matter. Let's face it. Those of us who have had children know that most of us *wished* that baby would come out long before it actually came out. But when it's time, and not a moment sooner or later, the brain sends a signal to the walls of the uterus to start contracting. What if that didn't happen? Eventually the child would outgrow its environment, and its environment would no longer be able to sustain it. That puts both baby and mother at risk.

Jesus was being "birthed" into His purpose. He had just been baptized by John, who called Him "the Lamb of God, which taketh away the sin of the world" (Jn. 1:29). The heavens had opened up and the Spirit of God descended like a dove and settled on Him. Then God Himself declared, "This is My beloved Son, in whom I am well pleased" (Mt. 3:17). It doesn't get better than that...and then the walls began to move.

We live our lives comfortably doing the will of God, serving in our churches, caring for our families, working "as unto God," keeping ourselves from uncleanness and fornication. We submit to the Word that tells us to forgive, pray, rejoice and worship. We are Spirit-filled, willing vessels. And God tells us in so many ways just how much He loves us...and then the walls begin to move. We lose our job. Our marriage falls apart or that man we were going to marry gets cold feet. What's that? Surgery? But there's no job, so there's no health insurance. The savings are gone. The house is in foreclosure. Folks at church see us "going through," so they stop calling, afraid they might be asked for a loan. And the ones who do stick around just want to know your business so they can have a little something to contribute to the "dish" that's going around about you. *I don't know how she got so broke. And she looks bad. She must be on drugs or something...* And there goes your reputation.

We're quick to say the devil is on our trail, but that's not always the case. Sometimes God has given the Holy Ghost a signal that it's time to birth you into another season. So the walls begin to move. The process can be violent and upsetting and confusing. The process can feel like betrayal, especially if it looks like everything God promised you is getting farther and farther away. The process can shake you to the foundation of who you are and put you on your knees in tears, unable to say anything but "Help me, Lord!" The process hurts. Oh, but on the other side...

Look at Luke 4:13. It says the devil "ended all the temptation [and] departed from Him for a season." Yes, the devil will be back when he thinks you're not ready. But the Word says the temptation ended, and he departed. "Weeping may endure for a night, but joy cometh in the morning," says Psalm 30:5b, and morning always comes. What happened for Jesus "in the morning" will happen for you too. Look at the very next verse, Luke 4:14: "And Jesus returned *in the power of the Spirit* into Galilee: and there went out a fame of Him through all the region round about." Jesus began His public ministry right after that wilderness experience. Notice that before the wilderness Jesus was "full of the Holy Ghost," and after it, He returned "in the power of the Spirit." Glory to God, He walked out of the wilderness and into the synagogue. That same Spirit that cast Him into the wilderness to suffer, gave Him power when He came out.

> *The Spirit of the Lord is upon Me, because He hath anointed Me to preach the gospel to the poor; He hath sent Me to heal the brokenhearted, to preach deliverance to the captives, and recovering of sight to the blind, to set at liberty them that are bruised, to preach the acceptable year of the Lord* (Luke 4:18-19).

The more you yield your vessel to each unction and urging of the Holy Spirit, the more power He makes available for you to do the good works that were ordained for you to walk in from the foundation of the earth (see Eph. 2:10). What wilderness has the Spirit led you into? How willing are you to go through it so He can birth you into your purpose? Do you know that there is power on the other side of where you are? There are poor souls waiting to hear the gospel from your lips. The brokenhearted await your healing touch. You have keys to set free those who are bound and chained to some of the same issues God set you free from in your wilderness. You are eyes for someone who can't see past their pain. You are balm for bruised and broken lives.

Powered By Power

Who are you? A better question is, who is God *in you*? Power is the ability and authority to recognize and reveal God. When you choose to become a daughter of the Father, a wife to the Son and a vessel of the Holy Spirit, you have made power your inheritance, your path and your guide. It becomes the means by which you live your life and the result of all that you do. When you live according to the will of God, God shows up, and power always shows up with Him.

Don't be fooled by counterfeits. Somebody may promise you "personal power," but it's not worth having if it doesn't include a personal relationship with God, the Lord Jesus and the Holy Ghost. You can try to access your "authentic power," but it will only be as "authentic" as your rusty, dusty, frail frame if the Way, the Truth and the Life is not its sum and substance. Every "path to love" must include the God who is love. Psychic hot lines won't keep you out of hell. The sting of Scorpio and the roar of Leo the Lion are worthless against the fiery darts of the enemy. (In fact, to the child of God, they *are* the fiery darts!)

God says His people perish for a lack of knowledge (see Hos. 4:6). To know God is to know His power, and that is salvation indeed.

From My Heart

As a wife, it's so easy to forget that I have a life separate from my husband's. But that truth hits me hardest when he's stressed. Then I reach for God, and He reminds me that I have the same power to give my mate that is found in my own personal relationship with Him as daughter, wife and vessel. I'd like to share a page from one of my journals with you:

Lord,

*So much of our lives is wrapped around the powerful, awesome assignment You entrusted to my husband. Today, strengthen **me** to put some of my petty desires and demands to the side and let me focus clearly, not on what he can do for me today, but rather what I can do for him today. What area of life have You given me influence, authority, power, wealth or prosperity that I can share in a positive way to affect his visions and his dreams?*

Lord, let me rise up in strength, so I can share that strength with him. Lord, empower me with courage—so in the face of his fears and defeat, I can transfer my courage to him and he never know about it. Jesus...he's tired, weary, worn...let me create a haven of rest, a room of peace, encouragement and joy that I can invite him into. Perhaps a day of solace and solitude is what I can give my husband today. A break from my critical, criticizing spirit. Let me put aside my neediness and help me embrace readiness to empower my man with support and resources that will benefit him personally and spiritually.

Father, I sense trouble, crisis and urgent needs. Help me dedicate the next 24 hours in prayer, praise and devotion as I seek understanding and wisdom to help my husband stand in his assignment, tall and fully equipped. Jesus...help me stand by him.

From Your Heart

Meditate on the following passages:

Before I formed thee in the belly I knew thee; and before thou camest forth out of the womb I sanctified thee...I have loved thee with an everlasting love: therefore with lovingkindness have I drawn thee. Behold, thou art fair, my love...fearfully and wonderfully made...Many daughters have done virtuously, but thou excellest them all...Abide in Me, and I in you. As the branch cannot bear fruit of itself, except it abide in the vine; no more can ye, except ye abide in Me...Follow Me.

How much of those passages do you believe? Where do you struggle? Write your thoughts below.

Chapter Two

Exercising Power

How awesome it must have been to witness Jesus during His ministry on earth. In just three short years the disciples watched Him heal the sick, raise the dead, restore sight to the blind, and cast out demons. He fed thousands with two fishes and five loaves, and those who ate missed the Miracle who was passing out Life as well with the evening meal. They watched Him command the storm to stop being a storm and sickness to stop making people sick. He declared a poor widow rich among prosperous people and showed a rich young ruler his poverty. His meat, He said, was to do the will of the Father, His Father. And they saw that same Father—who had twice tenderly called Him "beloved" from Heaven—turn from Him as He hung like a criminal from a cross.

They knew He was the Christ, the Messiah, and yet He washed their feet. The King of kings knelt like a slave and took their filthy feet in His hands, even the feet of the one who would betray Him. (In truth, they all betrayed Him. Judas was just the one who delivered Him into the hands of those who would crucify Him.) They saw Him die. They saw Him alive again. They saw Him ascend to Heaven. In three short years, John says Jesus did more than could fit in all the pages of all the books in the world (see Jn. 21:25). Still, as amazing as He was, Jesus told His disciples—and by extension you and me—that they would do even greater things than He (see Jn. 14:12).

And they did do greater things. Peter walked on water, raised people from the dead, healed the blind and the lame. Stephen died as Jesus did, begging God to forgive the people responsible. Paul was imprisoned, beaten, and would not complain. John saw the heavens open and beheld the glory of God as he received the book of The Revelation. So powerful was the impression Christ had made on their lives that all but one of them was martyred for His name's sake. The one who was not, John, lived a martyred life for the same cause. They served, loved and died for the glory of God, counting all loss as a blessing of fellowship with Christ. Why don't we walk in that same power?

Granted, times have changed. We are not thrown in prison for professing Christ, at least not in the United States.[1] But even in these times, how many people live their lives the way the apostles did, sold out for Jesus? If we're honest, that kind of life seems out of reach, unnecessary and a little strange to most of us. If Paul were alive today, we would call him "too spiritual." Peter would be "too intense." John's love for Jesus would be seen today as "needy" or "co-dependent." Jesus Himself probably would have a harder time of it now than He did back then. He wouldn't be hanging out with the television evangelists or the politicians. He'd be hiding from agents who had heard about the miracles and wanted to get Him His own talk show or negotiate a book deal. And can you imagine the rumors that would be going around about a single, virgin male who spends His time with hookers, criminals and homeless folks, and 12 guys who go everywhere with Him? He claims to be God in the flesh. He claims you can't get to God if you don't know Him. He claims He's going to die and come back to life! Would you believe Him? Would you follow Him? Would you die for Him? Would you live for Him?

1.　There are countries in the world where Christians are being persecuted still. There is a woman ministering in Africa whose family learned that she was a Christian and held a "funeral" as a declaration to the world that she was no longer alive to them. In some parts of Asia and the Middle East Christians are beaten, arrested and even killed for preaching and teaching the gospel.

Times have changed, but some things are still the same. In Jesus' day, He could not perform with great power where there was no faith. Faith moved mountains, healed issues of blood, gave sight, and calmed storms. But an entire town robbed itself of the power of Christ through unbelief. Today entire churches are powerless to help the people who walk through their doors because they do not believe. "I can do all things through Christ who strengthens me." How many times have you said this? How many times have you believed it? How many times have you doubted it?

God has given us power to live our lives. And we are content to do that—live *our* lives as we understand them to be. But did you ever consider that what God wants is not for us to just live our idea of our life, but to live *His* idea of our life? Faith is the evidence of things *not* seen. Eyes have not seen, ears have not heard, hearts have not dreamed the things that God has for those who love Him. (See Hebrews 11:1; 1 Corinthians 2:9.) You've seen money. You've heard the sound of a new car. You've dreamed of success, a husband, a thriving ministry. What *haven't* you seen? What *haven't* you imagined?

Bring the tithes into the storehouse and watch God open up the window of Heaven and pour out a blessing "that there shall not be room enough to receive it" (Mal. 3:10). You can receive millions. You can receive children, friends and a loving church. You can receive accolades and honor. You can receive that promotion, can't you? What is there in your life that you don't have room to receive? If you can imagine it, what God has for you is bigger than that. It's better than that.

We don't operate like the apostles did because we don't have the same perspective they did. Daily we ask God to join us as we believe for money, cars, houses, husbands to love us, husbands *that* love us, promotions and pretty figures. Stuff. Some of us even go so far as to pray for someone else to be healed from sickness, saved or protected from harm. Still stuff. We're believing God for *things*. If you really want to see God move, ask Him if you can believe what *He* believes. Ask to stand with Him on some things.

God said He knows the thoughts He thinks toward you. He also said His thoughts are not your thoughts. (See Jeremiah 29:11; Isaiah 55:8.) But He never said He would not share His thoughts with you. In fact, He says in Psalm 37 that if you delight yourself in Him, He will "give thee the desires of thine heart." That word *give* literally means to "place" into. In other words, He's willing to fill your heart up with what He wants you to want. Then He stands ready to give you everything you ask for.

So why don't we walk in more power than we do? Is it that we don't want it? Not likely. It's certainly not because He doesn't want us to have it. Paul tells us in Ephesians 1:18-23 that we should know that God has made available to us the same power He wrought in Jesus when He raised Him from the dead and set Him up in Heaven. So what's the problem?

Let's take a closer look at that passage in Ephesians. Paul is telling the Ephesians that his wish for them is that they would be enlightened so that they would truly understand what God wants to do in them, for them and through them. Look at verses 19 and 20:

> *And what is the exceeding greatness of His power to us-ward who believe, according to the working of His mighty power, which He wrought in Christ, when He raised Him from the dead, and set Him at His own right hand in the heavenly places.*

First of all, "to us-ward" actually means *into* us. Paul wants us to know the greatness of the power that God put into us who believe. But we believe, "according to the working" of that same power. In other words, God gives us the power to believe in His power. Then He gives us a picture of it. Paul says God worked His power in Jesus when He raised Him from the dead. So why aren't we walking in that same power? Because we are believing according to our power to believe, not according to God's power to believe *in us*. It's like we have a brand-new Ferrari in the garage, tuned up, fueled up and ready to go. But we've hitched it to a trailer that's attached to our Yugo, and we haul it around instead of driving it.

Wives are in loveless marriages with arrogant, insensitive, angry, women-hating men, refusing to use the power God gave them to transform that man into a strong, godly provider and protector, anxious to cherish and adore. Preachers refuse to tell the truth to stiff-necked congregations for fear of offending them instead of using the power of the Holy Spirit to level the strongholds of pride, unbelief and idolatry. Mothers won't use the power of the rod, then are shocked at their disrespectful, cruel, hateful, spoiled children. Single women defile their temples, shaming themselves and lying to the world about the power of God to keep you from evil. The power God has given to us to "overcome" is useless if we don't use it. Paul says God is able to do "exceeding abundantly above all that we ask or think, *according to the power that worketh in us*" (Eph. 3:20). If there's no power working in us, there's no power working for us.

Jesus said we would have power when the Holy Ghost came, to be witnesses unto Him (see Acts 1:8). A witness is someone who has information or knowledge about something and can give that information, bring that thing to light or confirm it in some way. We are supposed to be witnesses of Christ. People are supposed to be able to see the power God worked in Him working in us. We are supposed to live our lives in a way that tells the truth about who God is and what He can do. If we are witnesses unto Christ, we are witnesses unto power! We should have information about power, know power and confirm the power of Jesus Christ. And we do that according to the power God put in us.

Have you ever left your car sitting for a long time without driving it? Sometimes, if a car has been sitting unused for a period of time, it won't start because the battery is dead. You can lug that Ferrari around on that trailer if you want to. But one of these days, your "you-powered" Yugo is going to break down, and you'll have to drive it. And if you've been letting it sit, it might not start up right away. Thankfully, we can get a Holy Ghost "jump" if we need it. But if we get too far away from an adequate energy source, it can be very inconvenient, or even downright dangerous, especially if we're alone.

Power Corrupted

The power of God is nothing to play with. That's why we have a detailed instruction manual for owning and operating it. Everything we need to know about God and His power is there for us in the Bible, which, not surprisingly, requires God's power in us in order for us to understand it. But if we don't spend time with the Word in study or with the God who gave the Word in prayer; if we mishandle the Word in unbelief or become prideful in our understanding, what power we do have can become corrupted and therefore limited in its capacity to move in us and through us. Let's look at our definition of power again.

Power is the ability and authority to recognize or reveal God.

When we neglect to study the Word of God, we forsake the process by which God delivers our faith to us. "Faith cometh by hearing, and hearing by the word of God" (Rom 10:17). Then we *misuse* the power of God because we don't know how to *recognize* it.

A person who misuses the power of God is one who thinks she can't overcome her past or the agony of it. It is that woman who was raped and can't see herself allowing anyone to touch her ever again. It is that sister who has gotten a divorce and believes she's disqualified from ever having a loving, caring marriage. It is the preacher who thinks all sickness is a sin issue, so he doesn't know how to call on God as a Healer when his own child is sick. It's that brother whose unbelieving wife walked out on him two years ago, and he's still waiting for her to come back.

Sometimes we recognize that power is there for us, but we *refuse* it, declining to allow God to be *revealed* in and therefore through us. We do this when we're afraid of either failing or succeeding. It's easier sometimes to deal with the pain of what we know than to commit ourselves to the uncertainty of the unknown. You know why you're overweight. You know what you're eating even if you are doing it late at night when no one's around. You also know what you need to do. God has given you a path to follow and instructions on how to stay on that path. He has shown you in His Word that you can do all things. He has even put a girlfriend in your life who wants to go walking with you in the morning. But you won't get up. You won't call her back. You continue to reject every offer of help that the Spirit sends your way.

Satan is lying to you. He might be telling you that if you stay big, no one will violate you or hurt you again. Or he's saying you can't lose the weight at this point. Maybe he's saying the reason you don't have anybody is because you're big. And at the same time, he's plaguing your spirit with uncertainty. *What if you lose the weight and still don't have anybody? You'll have to say you don't have anybody because of who you are. And you can't change that.* So rather than have your greatest fear realized—that your destiny is to be unloved—you turn down God's offer of strength. But you should know, woman of God, that if you take God up on His offer, He'll show you every lie the enemy is telling you and has told you all your life. You'll see the real issues behind your weight, the real issues behind those drugs, that anger, that bulimia, that high blood pressure, or that low self-esteem.

Now, there are those who recognize God's power and acknowledge it. But they give it away to others and therefore *diffuse* it. When this happens, a person has surrendered the *authority* associated with power. God gave you a vision. You knew it was from God. You knew it was for you, because it spoke to a burden He placed in you years ago. But you took that vision and gave it to someone at your church with "more ministry experience" than you. Now they've turned it into something that you don't even recognize anymore. That was your vision. God had already set aside all the power you would need to bring that vision to pass. And you gave it away to someone without the call or the burden for it. And when you try to explain to them what it should be, they look at you like you're crazy. Why should you be telling them what it's supposed to be? It's not your vision anymore.

You saints who go to church on Sunday and shack up together for the rest of the week know what you're doing. The fact that you're getting married someday is not going to fly with God. You've given away your power as a witness because your life does not tell the truth about Jesus. He's holy, set aside, consecrated for use by God. You're being used by one another to fulfill your own desires.

Lastly, there are those men and women of God who corrupt their power through *abuse*. When you take your knowledge of God and His power and use it against people, you give up your *ability* to move in the fullness of it. God is love. When love is absent from your behavior, so is God and His power.

You can tell which saints are abusing their power. They're the ones who sit high and look low on all the other people who aren't as holy as they think they are. They look for position instead of positioning themselves to serve wherever they're needed. They'll talk about you for wearing your skirt too short in church and never stop to consider that those may be the only clothes you have in your closet. They cast stones at every passerby from the roofs of their glass houses.

Abusers are men of God who order their wives to obey them instead of modeling the submission Paul asks for from husbands and wives in Ephesians 5. Sunday in and Sunday out they preach, serve communion, teach, smile, greet and shake hands. Monday through Saturday their pseudo-sanctified demeanor turns surly and their wives feel the sting of their cruelty. They bark orders and seldom remember to say please or thank you. And if it looks like she—the one he was called to love as himself—wants to voice the slightest objection to his behavior, she's force-fed every Scripture on proper "wifery" contained in the Word until she's convinced that she's the heathen with the problem. Abusers of this sort don't care about the truth. They just care about being right.

And what about you, wife? Have you gotten so much Bible under your belt that you know more than your husband? How often do you let him know it? "I'm supposed to follow you? Hm! You don't even know where you're going!" They can hear you complaining about him all the way in the next county. You've stopped being a "W.I.F.E." (Warrior, Intercessor, Fortress, Equalizer) and now, in your diminished power, you've become a "w.i.f.e." (wicked, insensitive, fault-finding, emasculator). Your Bible may be big, but if it doesn't fall on your head and knock some sense into you, it won't do you much good.

Jesus saved His harshest criticism for the abusers of His time, the scribes and the Pharisees. They knew just enough Scripture to make them too blind to see the King. They used God's law to find a way out of their marriages instead of a way to reconciliation. Does that sound familiar in today's Church? They looked with disdain on Jesus for spending time with sinners. How diverse is the crowd you hang out with? Pastor, does your congregation look like an emergency room, or have your "saints" run all the sick souls away?

The Power of One

Single women are especially prone to misuse, refuse, diffuse and abuse power. This is due in part to the misrepresentation of women and their power in Scripture. We see the stories of Adam and Eve, Abraham and Sarah, Isaac and Rebekah, Moses and Zipporah, Ruth and Boaz, and so many other powerful couples. Then we are presented with the widows and women alone as tragic figures throughout the Bible. Add to that a society still struggling with issues of sexism and male dominance and a church culture that is in some ways behind society on those issues. It's no surprise that women not only buy into the lie that they have less power than men, but many women believe that their power will be found only when they have a man. Many single women are looking forward to marriage so they can "begin their ministry." Sister, do you not know that God made everything with a purpose? Your singleness was no exception.

In marriage a man and woman become "one flesh." Does this mean that before marriage they were each only half a person? Certainly not, and yet there is this misconception that a single woman has something to be ashamed of or that she's missing something that will "complete" her. Many of you are treating your single years as if you're in some sort of spiritual "holding cell," waiting for the Holy Ghost to come and call your number so you can walk down the aisle and become a "real woman." The unfortunate result of playing "The Waiting Game" in singleness is a lack of readiness for marriage.

In marriage you will have problems. Paul declared it so in the Word of God. There are things buried deep in the heart of every woman that only marriage will bring out because marriage goes to the core of your deepest fears and issues of trust and abandonment. But there is a lot of baggage we carry into marriage that we could have left in our singleness with a little shift in focus and some efforts toward contentment. The key to making yourself ready for marriage is to live your singleness to perfection. Perfection doesn't mean flawlessness; it means completeness. There is power in singleness that goes unused when we waste our time praying for marriage.

What is the power of singleness? It is the power to find your power. It is the power to press into the Almighty without distraction and discover the true Source of all your power and how to use it. It is the power to see all the debris left in your "temple" by your parents and your parents' parents; all that junk that makes you emotional, angry, hurt or afraid. It is the power to learn that no one is more important than God; to learn that He is your floor, ceiling and all the walls surrounding you. God's purpose for any single woman is that she be whole in body, mind and spirit. A single woman who's whole is one who knows, by experience, that God will never leave her or forsake her. That understanding alone is worth every year alone. Until you fully believe that God will not leave or forsake you, you cannot be married without some part of you—if even a small part—being desperately afraid of being left or rejected.

Finding your power in singleness means finding out you are God's woman. If you don't know that—if you spend your single season thinking you're "somebody's wife" in an incubator—you will not know how to seek God's will and His timing, or see His warning signals if something's wrong with the man you're about to give yourself to. When you neglect to live *into* the full power of your single season, you are forced to find out who you are within marriage. Then you can't be the most effective help meet for your husband, because you're too busy trying to "meet" yourself. Marriage is about two people serving one another. Serve your future husband now by serving God in your singleness.

We're All in This

Power is ours, woman of God. It is our birthright as daughters of the Father. It is the promise of our Husband, the King of kings. It is the gift of the Holy Spirit (see Acts 1:8). No one of us is more entitled than another, and none of us is exempt. In fact, a closer look at some of the women in Scripture reveals a God who was as gracious, if not more so, to women, especially those who struggled with loneliness, abandonment and immorality. There is no situation or circumstance that women deal with today that is not represented in the Word of God. You are in there, wife. You, too, single sister, mother, single mother, woman in ministry, executive, prostitute, virgin, diva and you with the shameful past. There are witnesses in Scripture excited to meet you and light a path at your feet.

Sarah: "Picture Imperfect" (Genesis 11:29–23:20)

Everybody's so sure you've got it all together—husband, children, security. But they don't know what it took to get where you are, or what it takes to stay there. He's the head, so what does that make you? You're the thing that supports the head. You're the backbone. Everything on the body is attached to you at some point. Every signal from the head to the body goes through you. Nothing moves without you, and yet, how much of what you do goes unnoticed, unacknowledged and unappreciated? Your husband does love you, but he doesn't always show it. In fact, sometimes he puts you in the frustrating position of having to pay for his mistakes and his weaknesses. Never mind that you're struggling with your own insecurity and fear.

But you know that your strength comes from a place that goes beyond every frailty of manhood, womanhood, motherhood and matrimony. You can't always be sure your family has a grip on God, but you know God has a grip on your family. You lift up your eyes unto the hills from whence comes your help... Help to clean up his messes and love him through them. Help to accept every apology. Help to ask him for forgiveness. Help to follow. Help to submit. Help to make up for your own lack. Help to give life to every dead and barren place in you and in your marriage. Help to bring you comfort, peace and love. You are a "princess," Sarah, and beloved heiress to His unspeakable joy.

Hagar: "Mistaken, Not Forsaken" (Genesis 16; 21:1-21)

Please don't pity me. I'm not as tragic as you think I am. What you see as the dishonor and shame of single motherhood has been the greatest of blessings to me. Yes, he's gone. Yes, he has another woman and other children. No, he doesn't support "me and mine." Yes, I've made mistakes. And yes, it's hard. But don't pity me. Because I have something Sarah doesn't.

The Lord has heard my cries and has come to see about me *personally.* Have you ever seen the Lord up close? I have, so many times. You've seen my kids. They're not hungry. They're not dirty. And they *know* they're loved! When they were little, I used to worry that I couldn't give them the best, because there was just me. The Lord heard my pain and came to me one day. He got real close to me and said, "Lift them up to me, Hagar. I'll make up the difference." And he has, so please don't pity me.

I have strength I never knew I had. I've seen a God I wouldn't have known if I had done everything right. And the truth is, everything is "right." I saw God up close when nobody else was there. And He hasn't left my side. I have everything I need...and everything I want, because I have hope.

Rahab: "That Was Then...This Is Now" (Joshua 2; 6:17)

Would you like to meet Rahab? It's really not that far to where she lives. In fact, she's pretty close—as close as your own mirror. We're all Rahab, woman of God; or at least we should hope we are.

Rahab was a prostitute. Most of us cannot imagine selling ourselves to anyone for money. Of course, some of us remember a time when we gave ourselves away for free. And all of us at one time or another has, through sin, sold ourselves to the devil for position, possession, comfort, security or accolades. And yet how many of us recognized salvation as quickly and as readily as Rahab? Do we discern the times and the seasons as well as she did? Surely we know these are the last days, but do we act according to that knowledge, with prudence and wisdom, as Rahab did?

Blessed is Rahab, because she is that woman who would not let her sin keep her from seeking salvation. Give honor where it is due. Rahab provided a safe place for Joshua's men. How safe is the Lord in your life? Is the Word hid in your heart the way those men were? Rahab knew that God was with them, and that power was also with them. She wisely chose to align herself with that power. They accepted her offer. They didn't think about the fact that she had a past. Her actions secured her future and the future of her whole family. You wife, how safely can you hide your husband's mistakes, failures and sins until the Lord finds and delivers him?

Your past does not disqualify you from receiving the protection and direction of the Savior. He's knocking. Let Him in. Make Him safe. Live.

Deborah: "You Go, Girl!" (Judges 4–5)

You are in charge. Or at least that's what they think...but you know better. You know who put you in that corner office on the top floor. The "Boys' Club"—the fellas who installed that glass ceiling you kept hitting your head on—never planned to let you in, but they didn't know there was One stronger than every roadblock they put in your path. They didn't know there was One higher than every head they tried to go over to keep you from getting ahead.

And now you're in their faces. Half of them have already started cleaning out their desks. But instead of bitterness, you greet them with a smile. "How can I best serve *you?*" is the first question you ask as their new boss. You praise them and encourage them as you direct them. You do all the things you wish they had done for you...because you know who put you where you are. And they follow you. They trust your judgment even if they don't like you, because you trusted in the One who said He would make your path straight and give you favor. Never forget who's the Boss.

The Widow of Zarephath: "Let Go...Let God" (1 Kings 17:8-24)

I hear your wailing, precious widow. Haven't I taken enough from you already? Your husband, your job, your health, your children's happiness, your joy, your dignity and your hope seemed unimportant to Me as I snatched them from you one by one. And what you have left, I have asked you for, too. But if you give Me everything, then you'll have nothing left to do but receive.

Everything I've done was for a reason. If you'll surrender the last of what you're holding onto, I will show you the power of creation. You see, no one can make something from nothing but Me. No one can make an empty heart full but Me. No one can bring water from a rock but Me. No one can make life spring from death but Me. I want to show you that miracle. And I want to duplicate that wonder in your life over and over again. So you see, I had to take everything. Fear not. Trust Me. Open up your hands and give Me everything. Then keep your hands stretched open toward Me...and watch as I begin to pour.

Abigail: "Life After the Fool" (1 Samuel 25:2-42)

Admit it. You married a fool. Was he a fool when you married him, or did he turn into a fool? Or were you too big a fool to pay attention at the time? It doesn't really matter. You married a fool, and everybody knew it. Nobody on earth would've blamed you if you had walked out on him. But you were not concerned with the opinions of anybody on earth. So you endured. Your Father in Heaven let you marry this crass, arrogant, selfish, inconsiderate, irresponsible, self-possessed, rude, ain't-even-trying-to-know-God, *clod*! He gave you what you asked for, and tried you in the flames of it.

You served him well. You loved him. You remained faithful to him and wouldn't allow anybody to talk about him. You defended him, protected him and put up with him without a word of complaint. Then he left you. As badly as he treated you, you had to suffer the humiliation of being the one "left." And because you never said anything bad about him, nobody's really sympathetic. Your friends are still his friends, and that hurts. He's picked up and moved on, but will you?

Don't worry, Abigail. God has seen your faithfulness to Him. And because you have honored His commandments, He will restore to you everything you lost. Don't think He won't come see about you.

The Woman at the Well: "Secret Shame" (John 4:1-42)

I didn't tell Jesus anything. I just started talking to Him, and He told me all about myself. There's so much that I have to be ashamed of, so much I've done. Actually, I'm still doing a lot of things. He knew that too. And you know what? He didn't condemn me. He just kept talking to me about living water and worshiping in Spirit and in truth. I didn't get the feeling that He was excusing me at all. But the way He talked, I felt—well, I felt *clean* for the first time in my life.

We talked about everything. The stuff my father did to me, and my uncles. The things I let people do to me now. The abortions. (Yeah, there was more than one.) I don't feel ashamed about it anymore. He said He loved me. You know, if He can love me like this, maybe there's hope for me. I'm so free, happy and excited...I must run and tell someone else.

Mary of Bethany: "Singular Sensation" (Luke 10:38-42; John 11:1-47; 12:1-8)

Single sister, if Jesus asked you to change your name to Mary, would you do it? If He wanted your undivided attention, could He get it for as long as He wanted it? Would you sit at His feet, rapt, oblivious to all but the words that fell from His lips? Would you ignore the urging of others who want you to devote yourself to "doing for" Jesus instead of the "being with" Jesus?

Single sister, can Jesus count on you to trust Him with your deepest fears? Does He know you'll wait on Him and believe while in your roughest storm? Would you still love Him if He showed up after the devastation instead of before it? Then, would you let Him lead you into another storm?

Single sister, if Jesus asked you to sacrifice the thing most dear to you for Him, would you do it? If He asked you to prepare the man you love for marriage...*to someone else*, would you do it with joy?

Single sister, how do you adorn your soul when you know you're going to meet Jesus in prayer or worship? Is He pleased to fill Himself with the fragrance of you? Do you remind Him of someone He used to know? Single sister, if Jesus asked you to change your name to Mary, *could* you do it?

Peter's Wife: "The Color of the Wind" (1 Peter 3:1-7)

You don't see the wind, but you know it's there, because you see the way other things are carried by it. Floating leaves, a seagull, the sail of a ship—if we look at them long enough, we eventually must acknowledge the wind.

They may never mention your name. Too often, you're no more than a mention in an introduction or a footnote in an article. To many, you are a pretty accessory, nice, but not really necessary. To a few, who try to catch the eye of the one you love, you're a placeholder, a bed warmer, the soon-to-be-ex-Mrs. So-and-so. But that's only because they can't really see you...but he does.

To him, you are the wind. You are the reason he can preach about a godly wife, even if he does use others as his examples. You are the reason he's strong enough to preach about anything! He is a man of power, covered by your powerful prayers. His confidence is nurtured in your arms. And as he allows God to take him, break him, bless him and feed him to the world, you are used of God to keep his spirit lifted and urge him on in his calling...like the wind.

Preachers, politicians, possessors of land, mothers of wayward sons and daughters of incest—they're all there. God has not forgotten the women who toil, or the women who wasted their youth. He has made mention of the wise, the foolish, the bitter, the angry and the dishonest, the sullied and saintly, the meek and contentious. He loves us all. And He offers Himself to us all, to adore us and to place in us His power.

It's impossible for a woman to define her power if she hasn't defined her relationship with the Almighty. Without that, any strength she has is carnal and "a form of godliness" at best. But once the "vertical" relationship is in order, she will recognize that power is not found in the things of this world or in her own efforts. Power comes from God, the Lord, Savior and Lover of our souls. Knowing that, she will not be so quick to surrender or mishandle His precious gift.

From My Heart

"Don't Let Your Backbone Slip!"

How did I end up in the emergency room? I told them I'd be okay, but my assistant and my daughter disagreed. I watched through half-closed eyelids as nurses buzzed around me. I wondered what was taking so long. I had so much to do. *Where's my phone? Somebody...bring my...calendar. I...should be...should...*

I was exhausted, plain and simple. For the next few days, I couldn't get out of bed for more than an hour at a time without feeling faint. I couldn't eat much, and what I did eat was hard to keep down. My daughter called her job to let them know she wouldn't be there. My husband was out of town. When he found out what happened, he got on a plane and came home. I was grateful. I wanted him with me. But you know what? I felt guilty too. Other people were adjusting their lives around me, and that's not the way it was supposed to be. I'm supposed do all the adjusting and bending. I felt powerless.

Then the Lord spoke to my heart. His power is the power to love. Would I deny that to my husband and my daughter? And is my love for them measured only by what I'm able to do for them?

List four people you love and serve regularly. Why are you grateful for them?

1._____ : _____

2._____ : _____

3._____ : _____

4._____ : _____

Take a moment to thank them personally and share what you wrote about them.

From Your Heart

Meditate on the following passages:

Abba Father!...be merciful unto me: heal my soul; for I have sinned against Thee. I am carnal, sold under sin...Fear not, for I am with thee...if thou wouldest believe, thou shouldest see the glory of God...I will instruct thee and teach thee...For we wrestle not against flesh and blood...But ye shall receive power...to stand against the wiles of the devil...In returning and rest shall ye be saved...because greater is He that is in you, than he that is in the world.

1. Write about the last sin you struggled with committing. What was your struggle?

_____

_____

_____

2. What could you say now that might keep another from committing the same sin?

_____

_____

_____

_____

3. What could you say now to comfort another who has committed the same sin?

_____

_____

_____

_____

Powering Forward...

Understanding the concept of power and what it means to be a woman behind the power of God is only the first step in truly operating in it. The next five chapters of this book are devoted to practical application of the things we've looked at so far.

Throughout the Bible, men and women have been reborn and transformed by the power of God. That process always begins with God, moves to the heart of the person, and then to that person's mind. The change in behavior that results from that process opens the door to a powerful demonstration of God's glory in and around that individual.

We're going to follow the same pattern and path to God's power in the remaining chapters of this book. First, we will examine the necessary *desire* to perceive, possess and protect the power of God, then *discern* the omniscience, omnipresence and omnipotence of God. We will look at the requirement to devote ourselves to the Word, works and worship. This leads us to exodus, exchange and excess. Finally, our lives become a declaration that revelation + response = rest.

Perceive	Possess	Protect
Omniscience	Omnipresence	Omnipotence
Word	Works	Worship
Exodus	Exchange	Excess
Revelation	Response	Rest

Are you ready to access your power?

Chapter Three

Perceive It...Possess It...Protect It

The path to power begins with our desire to see it, own it and hold onto it. But before we can understand what it means to *perceive it*, *possess it* and *protect it*, we must grasp the essence and elements of *desire*. Desire moves us to make choices, both good and bad. If we don't look at desire and learn the truth about it, we can't be free from making bad choices, or be free *to* make good ones. In other words, we won't be able to choose God or His power.

Fire and Desire

You've seen it. If you haven't seen it, you've heard about it. The man of God is preaching powerfully, delivering souls and slaying demons left and right. The Word is going forth Sunday after Sunday. Lives are changing. God is glorified in the beauty of the holiness of His people. Then satan sends his weapon of destruction into that house. She graciously takes a seat in the back, but on the aisle so the preacher has to pass her on his way out after service. She stands and her lap scarf slides to the floor. Pastor—always the gentleman—picks it up and gives it to her. Both her hands gently grasp his hand and, with a look that does not include anyone around him, gushes shyly, "Pastor, you blessed me so. This is my first time here. If I had known the Word was going forth like this, I would have visited a lot sooner." Translation: "If you'd like your ego stroked like this every Sunday, invite me back." Of course, he does.

She sits a little closer to the front next time, and the next time closer still. Soon she's involved in ministry, volunteering wherever she can—"Wherever Pastor needs me." Six months later Pastor is leaving his wife and kids, and everybody who's saying they're shocked ain't really shocked. When sin like that is born in a church, there are a lot of silent midwives helping it along. But where was that sin *conceived*?

The Book of James says sin didn't just spring up when that sister's skirt crept up her leg during service. And it didn't begin that first night the two of them spent in his hotel room while his wife was at home praying traveling grace over him. James says sin is conceived in our own *desire*—desire that was in that man before he ever laid eyes on that woman, and desire that was in that woman before she ever set foot in that church. "But each one is tempted when he is drawn away by his own desires and enticed. Then, when desire has conceived, it gives birth to sin; and sin, when it is full-grown, brings forth death" (Jas. 1:14-15 NKJ).

Now, we know that in order for a woman to conceive a child, something outside her has to enter her. Sin is born in desire the same way. Look at the passage again. Man (or woman) is "drawn away by his own desires and enticed." Right after that, there's conception. So what was the "sperm" that entered and coupled with desire to bring forth sin? The word *entice* comes from a Greek root that means "to decoy" or "to entrap." What do decoys and traps have in common? Lies. And you know who is the father of all lies. In other words, our desires commingle with a lie that we believe (because a lie has no power if we don't believe it), and sin is born.

That pastor believed the lie that it was all right to fantasize about that woman. That woman believed her desire to have a man meant it was okay to have any man or *anybody's* man. And lies always travel in packs. Each one is attached to a bunch of other lies: One time won't hurt anybody. His wife doesn't understand him like I do. Nobody knows what's going on. God understands my needs. My wife drove me to this woman. He loves me, and he would never do to me what he did to his first wife. (The bonus lie: She was his third wife, sweetheart).

Paul says that we've been powerless against our desires since Adam and Eve messed up in the Garden. He says we're so messed up that we can't do right even when we want to do right, and we can't keep from doing wrong even when we don't want to. Then along comes Jesus. "Behold," He says, "I stand at the door, and knock: if any man hear My voice, and open the door, I will come in to him, and will sup with him, and he with Me" (Rev. 3:20).

This is an invitation to Life as opposed to death, to Light instead of darkness. What happens, though, between hearing Christ's voice and opening the door? Desire. But the difference this time is we are not enticed by lies; we are entreated by the Truth. When we believe that truth (because truth has no power unless it is believed), it comes in and commingles with our desires. And when our desire conceives, it brings forth holiness. Then when holiness is full-grown, it brings forth eternal life. James 1:18 says, "Of [God's] own will begat He us with the word of truth, that we should be a kind of firstfruits of His creatures." The firstfruits of anything is holy and consecrated unto God, set aside by His command, for His use and His good pleasure.

What are your desires? What do you see that you think you can't live without? And what lies are you allowing to mix with your desires? Do you desire financial stability and believe the only way you can get it is to cheat on your taxes? Do you desire acceptance and believe the lie that you have to keep your relationship with Jesus low-key so you don't offend your unbelieving friends? Do you desire your husband to apologize for hurting you and believe that withholding sex will make him "sorry"? Do you desire holiness and believe that you are holy as long as nobody from church sees your pornography collection?

The desires, or lust, that James talks about is the result of our sin nature. That nature distorts our desires. But when Jesus enters the picture, He shows us the truth about ourselves and tells us to make a choice. Choose Him, or choose yourself. Choose life, or choose death. But Jesus also says no one even comes to Him unless the Spirit draws him (see Jn. 6:44). The Holy Spirit literally "drags" us "to a certain point": that point being the truth. Then we decide if we will open the door and let the truth in. So the Spirit gets us to Jesus, and Jesus gets us to the Father. In other words, you need power, to bring you to the power that leads you to *the* power...but only if you desire it.

God will give you everything you need to make the right choice, but He won't make you make the right choice. He will lead you to the Living Water, but He will not make you drink it. You have to desire His power before He'll give it to you. He's not going to sneak it into your coffee or sprinkle it on you while you sleep. You have to desire it, without shame, without hesitating. And when God sees your desire for Him, He will bust a hole in the clouds and pour it out on you, without shame, without hesitation, in the presence of your enemies—both the ones you know and the ones you don't know.

How do we know when our desire has pleased God enough to grant us our petitions? We look to the One He sent to us as an example. We look to Jesus. Don't you remember Him telling you to take His yoke upon you and "learn of Me"? Learn to serve one another like He did. Learn to cry out to God like He did. Learn to think the way He thought. Mostly, learn to want the things Jesus wanted, the way He wanted them. In terms of desiring God's power, that means we have to desire to perceive power the way Jesus did, desire to possess it the way Jesus did, and desire to protect it the way He did.

Perceiving Is Believing

Jesus perceived the power of God the way He perceived all things, through the eyes of faith. Faith is not "seeing something that isn't there." Faith is "not seeing something that *is* there." The writer of Hebrews says faith is the substance of things hoped for and the evidence of things not seen (see Heb. 11:1). No man has seen God, and yet throughout the Bible we see men and women follow Him, do battle with Him, stand before kings in His name, build up, tear down, move, wait, dance and pray—all for His glory. A six hundred-year-old man named Noah built a boat on dry land for his unseen Foreman. Abram was told to leave his home and go to a land that this now unseen Guide *would show* him. Mary praised God for the Savior before His birth, before the first miracle, before the cross, and before the resurrection.

Jesus said nobody born of a woman was greater than John the Baptist. Malachi prophesied John's coming as God's messenger sent to prepare the way before the Lord. Isaiah announced his coming as "the voice of one crying in the wilderness." You remember John the Baptist—the man born of a barren woman and a temple servant, born to decrease that Jesus the Christ might increase. John is God's finest example of the power of God seen through the eyes of faith. Isaiah declared his coming in grand fashion in Isaiah 40:1-4 among his words of comforting exhortation to Jerusalem. Then Matthew, Mark, Luke, John and John the Baptist himself confirmed that prophecy. Look at Luke 3:4-6:

> *As it is written in the book of the words of [Isaiah] the prophet, saying, The voice of one crying in the wilderness, Prepare ye the way of the Lord, make His paths straight. Every valley shall be filled, and every mountain and hill shall be brought low; and the crooked shall be made straight, and the rough ways shall be made smooth.*

These dramatic words paint a picture of a revolutionary new Kingdom, one that doesn't look like anything we're used to seeing. A Kingdom of filled valleys, leveled mountains, straightened curves and smoothed bumps. Author Donald B. Kraybill called it *The Upside-Down Kingdom.* The thing that distinguishes this Kingdom from those before it is that with its coming, everything as the world knew it and understood it would be flipped, switched, turned around and turned over into something unimaginable. Old ways would be altered so drastically that they wouldn't be recognized. The King who would come to run this Kingdom was "upside down" just like His Kingdom. And John the Baptist saw it.

In fact, John saw the coming Kingdom so clearly that he devoted his life to heralding it. He walked around in scratchy, furry clothes, eating bugs and honey and crying out to anyone who would listen, "Hey! Repent! The Messiah is gonna be here any day now!" Can you imagine how strange he must've looked to people? But people got saved listening to John. Think about that. John was leading people to a Christ who hadn't even shown up yet. Some of us can't lead somebody to a Christ who's already resurrected!

What drove John? What drove people to John? What gave him the courage to talk about something nobody else was talking about, in a way that nobody was talking about it? All the preaching in those days took place at the temple. But John was in the wilderness. Are there anymore "wilderness preachers" in the world today? Are there any willing to go where "proper people" don't go to hear the gospel? Can you put down your St. John suits, your Platinum charge, and your Ritz-Carlton Sunday brunches long enough to see what the wilderness looks like through the tinted windows of your S-class Mercedes?

Oh, to see the way John saw! He preached a Kingdom that hadn't come. And what he preached was like nothing that had ever been preached before that time. Yet, when it came, he recognized it. "Behold," he shouted, "the Lamb of God, which taketh away the sin of the world. This is He of whom I said, After me cometh a man which is preferred before me: for He was before me. And I knew Him not: but that He should be made manifest to Israel, therefore am I come baptizing with water" (Jn. 1:29-31).

John's destiny was to look for Jesus, and when he saw Him to say, "This is the guy!" John's purpose on earth was to recognize "power," and it took power to do that. The Bible says he was filled with the Holy Spirit in his mother's womb. That Spirit jumped inside Elizabeth when Mary walked through the door pregnant with power. Then that same Spirit carried him through every moment of his life until he saw the reason for his rejoicing again. And because he saw by the power of that Spirit, he knew his place in the invisible, unimaginable Kingdom he spent his life preaching about. How many of us would be content to decrease after all those years of obscurity and solitude in the wilderness? Most of us would want to begin a whole new "I Told You So" ministry, with better clothes, better food and the personal endorsement of the Messiah Himself. We might ask Him to put His name on all our posters and fliers. "Jesus the Christ Presents: Elijah II, the Prophet Returns!" or "Official Herald of the King of Kings," or something like that. But John was just happy to see Him.

We ought to work on our "just happy to see Him" ministry. Then we'll truly perceive things the way Jesus did. In the morning, just happy to see Him. At noon, just happy to see Him. In the evening...you've got it: Just happy to see Him. Jesus said, "Seek the Kingdom of God." In other words, live like John did, looking for that Kingdom to come. If you keep looking long enough, you'll begin to see things the way Jesus saw them—upside down.

When we see through the eyes of faith, our whole perspective changes. Our point of view becomes the viewpoint of the Branch who is also the Root, the Shepherd who is also the Lamb, the Bread and the Water, Alpha and Omega, Author and Finisher, King and Servant, God and Man. When we see things like He sees them, we decrease to increase. We give to receive, die to live and serve to rule. Our understanding embraces what is foolishness to man as wisdom from God. Poverty is prosperity, failure becomes success, persecution is a blessing. We learn to return good for evil, become low to be exalted and hungry to be filled. We see by faith, and faith comes by hearing, so we hear in order to see.

It's no surprise then that power doesn't look like power as we know it. The Jews expected the Messiah to come kicking in the door and flinging Romans left and right. They wanted Him to charge in on His white steed, chariots blazing. They wanted the Lion of Judah to rip their enemies to pieces. Instead, they got Joseph's boy. *You know Joseph, the guy who got that girl pregnant before they got married? The carpenter from Nazareth. You know his wife Mary is related to Elizabeth, the mother of that crazy guy...the one who eats the bugs out in the wilderness. Um-hm. He's supposed to be the Savior of the world? But He's got no power!*

Oh, if they could have seen what John saw! They would have seen power in His humility, power in the way He handled the Holy Scriptures, power in His kindness and power in His willingness to give all glory to God. If they had seen power the way Jesus saw it, they would have known that it took all He had to take off His glory and put it away so He could become a simple man. They would have seen His power on the cross where He hung, forsaken by the One who had loved Him since before the world was formed. And they would have believed He had risen when they saw the stone rolled away from His tomb. If they had seen with the eyes of Jesus, they would have seen the Truth and been set free.

Woman of God, what you see is not the last word on your life. You see a husband who's cold and distant. But did you hear God say he can be changed by your behavior? Did you hear him warn your husband to treat you right, or his prayers would be hindered?

(See 1 Peter 3:1-7.) You see the saints condemning you and talking behind your back. Have you heard that no weapon formed against you would prosper and that every one of those tongues will be condemned by you? (See Isaiah 54:17.) You saw those drugs in your son's sock drawer, but listen when God tells you that if you raised him according to the Word, he'll straighten up. (See Proverbs 22:6.) Your power is not in what you see with your eyes, but what you see in the Spirit—and the Spirit is Truth.

When God formed "Calling First Ladies"—a ministry of renewal, restoration and resource for wives of pastors, doctors, politicians, athletes and entertainers—the enemy had been showing the world that there were no guarantees for high-profile marriages. Husbands continued to fall prey to adultery, pornography, abuse and anger. Wives floundered helplessly in their own anger, bitterness and shrewish behavior. But God said in His Word that marriages—all marriages—were ordained to be an illustration to the world of His promise to redeem, restore and renew His people. The enemy had women and men resigned to accepting or rejecting their shattered unions. But spiritual eyes see the power that can be wrought in any marriage where at least one person loves the Lord and is willing to walk by faith.

All over this country, God is giving a word to women of faith to deliver to a world of depressed and hopeless souls. God is saying, "I see your desolation. I see your tears. I see your poverty. Now hear Me when I tell you that you are My woman. You will mount up on wings as eagles. You can do all things. I want you to prosper. I will fill every void in you and around you. This is not your last chance. You do have worth. You are not damaged goods. I do love you."

Hear what God is saying, sister. Then see it. Put it before you as you walk through the valley of the shadow of death, reminding yourself that it is only the *shadow* of death. You have eternal life. Focus on it as you face every trial ordered into your life to perfect you. Jesus endured the cross "for the joy that was set before Him" (Heb. 12:2). Has God put some joy before you? Are you focused on it? Look at that loving marriage, those healthy children, that thriving ministry, that day when you will hear Him say, "Well done, good and faithful servant. Well done."

Possessed Power

Have you ever thought about what a ridiculous name we've given the food processor? To "process" something is to put it through an orderly or established series of steps or operations toward a desired result. Sure, we get the desired results with a food processor. Whatever we put in gets ground, smashed, pulverized, blended or stirred. But there's really no order to it, no established series of steps beyond pushing a button, and after a few seconds of "*Vvwheeeeee*" removing the blades and scraping the gooey sides of a plastic cylinder.

That's not unlike our society when you think about it. We are result seekers, unconcerned with steps, ordered or otherwise. We worship at the altar of "done" without paying our respects at the laver of "doing." We're the "microwave generation, "Generation Now." We don't want to wait for anything or wait through anything. We want the weight off, but we don't want to go through the process of actually losing it. We reward our kids for good grades, but do we spend as much time applauding them while they're working to get the grades?

A brilliant scientist was once asked how he became so exceptional at research. He said, "It was my mother, really. When I came home from school as a child, she never wanted to see my grades. She only wanted to know if I had asked any good questions. It became a goal of mine every day to impress her with how inquisitive I could be." When was the last time you studied how your child studies?

When we forsake process, we may gain time, but we lose a lot more. If we were building a house, skipping process would be like laying down a floor without a foundation, putting up the walls without support beams, then setting a roof on top of it without nails. It will look like a house. It might even impress the neighbors. But don't let the wind blow or the rain fall. You'll end up with a pile of mess. When it comes to possessing power, the same principle holds true. Seeking the result without going through process may save you some time, but it will cost you more in the long run.

As faith underpins perception, so process is the floor of effective possession. In other words, if you want to possess power the way Jesus possessed it, you have to go through the process He went through. Think of it like buying a car. You may "have" it when you drive it off the lot, but it's not really "yours" for another 36 or 48 or 60 months. If during that time you stop making your payments, that car can be taken away from you.

Power was "perfected" in Jesus while He was in the world. He had to go through some things. He had to conquer some temptations, resist some sin and forgive some folks. And every time He overcame, He got stronger. As He suffered with obedience, God gave Him more and more power until He was able to stand with His disciples in Matthew 28:18 and say, "All power is given unto Me in heaven and in earth." That "power" is the Greek word *exousia*, which speaks of a power that "denies the presence of a hindrance" and connotes both authority and ability to do anything.

Jesus didn't have that perfected power when He came out of the womb. He didn't have it when He preached in the temple as a child. His power was given to Him portion by portion as He went through the excruciating process ordained for Him before the foundation of the world. The writer of Hebrews says He went through that process so He would have the power to save us, then have the power to be able to comfort us as we go through whatever process God has ordained for us (see Heb. 2:14-18). You do know that your life is already plotted out for you? Take a look at Psalm 139:16. The New Living Translation says, "You saw me before I was born. Every day of my life was recorded in your book. Every moment was laid out before a single day had passed." Our ending was known before our genesis. In fact, the life we now live is really a re-run for God, who planned and plotted every second of it before a second of it came into being. So nothing that's happening to you is a surprise to Him.

Wouldn't it be nice if God, knowing that we belong to Him, could just snatch us up so we wouldn't have to go through anything else on this earth? We could avoid whatever sickness and sin was waiting for us around the corner. We wouldn't have to die. But God wants to perfect us just like He perfected Jesus. And since we know that Jesus, having suffered more than we ever will, is sitting on the right hand of the Father, complete and possessing all power, we know that we can possess power the way He did if we are willing to pick up our cross and follow Him.

God only gives us as much of anything as we can handle. He only gives us as much sorrow, as much money, as many friends as we can take care of. Nothing more. He's the same way with power; He only gives us as much as we can deal with. David was a teenager when Samuel anointed him as king. But it was 17 years before David would sit on a throne. God had to take him through some stuff to strengthen him so he'd be able to keep it.

Take a look at Philippians 2: 5-10:

> *Let this mind be in you, which was also in Christ Jesus: who, being in the form of God, thought it not robbery to be equal with God: but made Himself of no reputation, and took upon Him the form of a servant, and was made in the likeness of men: and being found in fashion as a man, He humbled Himself, and became obedient unto death, even the death of the cross. Wherefore God also hath highly exalted Him, and given Him a name which is above every name: that at the name of Jesus every knee should bow, of things in heaven, and things in earth, and things under the earth.*

This is the story of the Savior in a nutshell. But it is also the blueprint for possessing power in and through process. There are four steps involved. They are as follows: 1) *Giving Up*, 2) *Giving In*, 3) *Standing Under*, and 4) *Understanding*.

"Giving Up" is a picture of submission. Philippians 2:6-7 says Jesus was equal to God and made a conscious choice to make Himself "of no reputation, and took upon Him the form of a servant... in the likeness of men." Theologians spend a lot of time debating what is meant by "equal" and "form" and "likeness." But take a moment to consider something else. Jesus knew who He was. He was everything, and He gave it all up to become nobody. He had a perfect relationship with God, and He gave it up. He was holy—had known only holiness—and He gave it up to live among the filth of sin. Can you imagine leaving your home, your family and your work to climb into a sewer to live for a season in waste? What Jesus did was more extreme than that.

Submission is simply "lining up" under an already established order. Wives, you do that every time you allow your husband to lead you. You are submitting, not just to him, but to God. In fact, if you're not submitted to God, then at best you're giving your husband lip service, and your "chaste behavior" is no more than a cloak for your rebellious heart. Single women, you submit when you honor that supervisor at work. Church volunteer, when you go through a ministry leader with your concern instead of picking up the phone to call the pastor directly, you have submitted.

"Giving In" is a picture of humility. Paul says Jesus humbled Himself and became obedient. It's easy to assume that obedience was no big deal to Jesus since He never complained. But the Scripture says He was obedient "unto death." How hard it must've been to "give in" and obey God and honor the order that was set up on earth when He knew who He really was. Yet if God said to sail to Gadarene, Jesus couldn't just snap His fingers and find Himself there. He had to sleep in the hull of the ship during a storm so God could have the disciples see Him speak to the wind. He had to wait until His friend Lazarus was dead before He went to him. He had to see all the anguish it caused Mary and Martha. Even He wept. But it had to happen that way so that God would be glorified and Jesus would be able to talk of His own resurrection. And He had to go to the cross. Scripture says He asked God if there was any other way to do what He needed to do (see Mt. 26:39-44). But it was when He gave in and said, "Nevertheless not My will, but Thine, be done," that God sent an angel to give Him another measure of power to handle the cross (Luke 22:42-43).

That measure of power made it possible for Jesus to "Stand Under" the pressure of His circumstances. This is the picture of patience. Patience is the ability to wait with wisdom. Wisdom takes knowledge, attaches the Word of God to it, does what it can, and doesn't move until God shows up with more instructions. Patience is faith, submission, humility and obedience combined. Look at Jesus in the wilderness with satan. Satan did not offer Him anything He couldn't have right there. He could turn stones to bread. He would be caught by angels if He had jumped from the top of the temple. He would one day own all the kingdoms of the earth. Why not now? Because that would have meant a crown with no cross—and the cross was why He came. So He patiently waited to be fed. He patiently waited to be validated by His Father in Heaven. And He patiently awaits the day when He will reign on earth.

Finally, and arguably the most important element in possessing power is "Understanding." The one who understands is the one who has peace. Peace is not just the absence of sound. It is the absence of the wrong sounds. Peace is understanding without frustration. Peace makes it possible to see everything falling apart and hear God in the midst of it saying, "Worry for nothing, precious child."

In peace we hear God. Paul tells us not to worry about anything, but to pray about everything, in Philippians 4:6. He tells us to make our requests known to God. Then he says in 4:7 that "the peace of God...shall keep your hearts and minds." If verse 6 says, "Tell God everything you need," you expect verse 7 to say you'll get everything you asked for. But it doesn't. It says, "Tell God what you need, and He'll give you peace." That's because peace makes it possible to hear Him say, "Be patient. I'm preparing you for what I have prepared for you."

What have you been praying about? Have you gotten peace about it yet? It doesn't matter how your family is acting up. If you have peace, you can get through it. It doesn't matter how high your bills are stacked. They can't be stacked so high that God can't see them. He will take care of them. But have you received your peace yet? Yes, that job needs to come soon. And that promise of a husband seems so far away. But have you checked your mail from the Father? He sent you some peace. Take it. Hold onto it. It's His assurance that you can wait for anything, endure anything, understand anything. It's His assurance that you have overcome the world.

When submission, humility, patience and peace combine with a thankful heart, contentment flowers in us. Contentment is that state of being that doesn't come from circumstances; it comes from knowing the God who holds all our times in His hands. Contentment is a choice we make to water every good thing growing in our lives and pull up every evil thing...today. Contentment doesn't dwell in regrets about yesterday or become anxious about tomorrow. Contentment says simply that this is the day that the Lord has made and that's enough reason to rejoice.

Paul says that he learned to be content in all circumstances, good and bad. He says it really doesn't matter what's going on, because he knows that God will always supply him with what he needs in a given situation. Paul went through the process of becoming content through submission, humility, patience and the pursuit of peace. And do you know what it got him?

I can do all things through Christ which strengtheneth me (Philippians 4:13).

That's right. He got power. But not just some power to do some things. He got complete power to do all things. God is thorough when it comes to taking care of His children. We just have to be willing to go through the process.

Protected Power

Once you perceive the power of God through the eyes of faith and possess that power through God's ordained process, you're obligated to protect its place in you through the discipline of devotion. Devotion is comprised of the disciplines of solitude, prayer and the study of the Word of God. Together these three act as a spiritual cleaning and maintenance system designed to protect your power from the things that would corrode it, inhibit its performance, shut it down, allow somebody to take it or render you unauthorized to use it.

You've seen part of your destiny. You've seen some of what God wants to do with you, for you and through you. You know what He's already doing in you. Your enemies see it too. Satan sees it. They all want you stopped, but they know that they can't stop you. They can't take away your promise. They can't rob you of your future. They know they can't take your power...but they know you can lose it.

We can lose our power when we get confused about how and when to exercise it. We can also lose it when we're too tired to hold onto it. It takes strength, courage and determination to move toward your destiny. Yet every time you take a step forward, it seems the forces of darkness are there to try to knock you down. Think it not strange, sister. You need to understand that *you are a target*. Your husband has been trusted with the mysteries of the Kingdom. *You are a target*. Your teenager is anointed to heal the sick, defend the helpless, topple corrupt governments and snatch other teens from the jaws of the devourer. *You are a target*.

You have watched the Word of God unfold before you—the wisdom of Eternity becoming your wisdom—and God has shown you the captives He has called you to set free. *You are a target.* You pray silently over every first grader you teach, and the Holy Spirit has shown you doctors, architects, inventors, preachers, congresspersons, scientists, movie stars, professional athletes and CEO's. *You are a target.* You're one year away from meeting the man who will be your husband, and God has prepared you to raise a child with the spirit and mantle of a prophet like Elijah. *You are a target.* You worship the Lord, set your affections on Him, follow hard after Him, seek to know the secrets of His heart. *You are a target.* And every once in awhile, you'll get knocked down.

What knocked you down? What challenge, crisis, circumstance, problem, person, place or thing knocked you down? Paul put it like this: "Ye did run well; who did hinder you that ye should not obey the truth?" (Gal. 5:7) What truth? The truth that God established when He declared your ending from your beginning. When He defined you, called you, sanctified you, ordained you and qualified you to walk into your destiny. What did you allow to hinder you? The New Living Translation says it like this: "You were getting along so well. Who has interfered with you to hold you back from following the truth?" In other words, what knocked you down? What prevented your growth? What stopped you? *What took your power?* There's only one answer. A lie took your power. A lie told you that you couldn't go on anymore. A lie told you that it wasn't worth it to keep on keeping on. A lie told you to throw in the towel.

The father of lies will throw every lie he can at you to try to knock you down and eventually knock you out. He's been lying to us since he opened his mouth in Eden, and he hasn't changed his tactics because his goal hasn't changed. He's out to "steal, kill and destroy." So settle it right now. He's going to lie to you every chance he gets. But a lie only has power when we believe it over the truth, or when we believe it because there is no truth to compare it to. Devotion is caring for the Spirit of God within you, that Spirit being the Spirit of truth (see Jn. 16:13).

The Spirit is the same Spirit given to us when we receive Christ. It is the Holy Spirit, which is also our power. Our power is found in the way we receive, perceive and believe the truth. When we neglect our spirit by receiving and believing lies, we diminish our capacity to protect the truth and, by extension, the power we've been given from God. Devotion—solitude, prayer and study—is a greenhouse for the truth. It receives the seeds of truth, plants the truth in good soil, waters the truth and provides a nurturing, safe environment for it to grow.

Solitude is not simply time spent alone. Solitude is separation from the world. When we seek solitude, we pull the cord on our connection to the things of the world. That doesn't mean we ignore our position as mother, employee, friend, sister, wife, group leader, etc. That's not solitude. That's isolation. Solitude is a conscious effort to place the whole of yourself before God. It's not just putting your body there, but also your mind and your spirit. Everything you think about yourself, apart from what you think about others, is brought into solitude. How you feel about yourself, away from the memory of what others have said about you, is carted into solitude with you. Obligations aren't a part of solitude beyond their part in defining you. For instance, motherhood is a part of who you are, so you bring it. Mentally arranging your day to accommodate your daughter's play date stays outside of it.

The purpose of solitude is to invite the truth to be seen. The truth is we are not supposed to carve time with God out of our busy lives. We're supposed to carve a life out of our time with God. Author Henri Nouwen, in his book *Out of Solitude*, focuses our attention on Mark 1:32-39. There we find Jesus healing the sick, casting out demons and dealing with crowds of people. Later in the passage He's preaching and casting out demons in the neighboring towns and teaching in their synagogues. Nestled among all that "busy-ness" is Mark 1:35:

> *And in the morning, rising up a great while before day, He went out, and departed into a solitary place, and there prayed.*

How often do you "depart" into solitude? Solitude is an essential part of every Spirit-filled life. It's not how we spend our time apart from our ministering. Solitude is where we find our ministry. It's where we draw the line in the sand with the enemy, declaring our enmity with him and our friendship with God. Solitude is not an option. Neglect it, and you quench the Spirit.

In solitude you hear God. The words of comfort He longs to say are heard in solitude. The sweet reassurances that you are His precious child, His cherished bride, and His lovingly crafted vessel are heard in solitude. God gets real specific in solitude. *You* matter to Him there. *You* have His full attention there. He is *your* Shepherd, *your* refuge, *your* soul's Lover, *your* King.

Solitude is also a place to discern the voice of God. In solitude, the enemy may speak to you. You may even try to sabotage your own soul with discouraging words. But in solitude, the words of God are clarion gifts, designed to refresh, renew and restore you. All other voices in you submit to the truth of what's being said by God. So anger, bitterness, discontentment, pride, rebellion, vanity, fear, unrest and unforgiveness become naked in your solitude, because darkness can't exist where there is light. When you invite yourself to be lit by the Spirit of God in your solitude, He will show you all that's in your heart. And the heart that Jeremiah calls deceitful and wicked cannot lie successfully in the face of God (see Jer. 17:9).

Prayer is your response to all that you find in solitude. Thanksgiving, uncertainty, sorrow, adoration, inquiry and disappointment are all expressed through prayer. Prayer is more than just a conversation with God; it is the longing of your soul stretching up to meet Him, intensely desiring to feel His presence, be understood and experience His love. We don't pray just to hear ourselves talk. We pray so that God will hear us. How many times are your prayers accompanied by an intense desire to be heard, understood and accepted? Most of our prayers only go as high as the ceiling because that's all the passion we put into them.

When prayer is born of simple lust, it becomes sickly and diseased. James says such prayers are petitions "prayed amiss." But when we pray from a place of truth, we know that God hears us. We'd be surprised to find out how many of our prayers contain lies. "Lord, I can't stay in this loveless marriage any longer." God is love. If He's in one of you, then love is there. Now if what you prayed is the truth, that means God was not in you when you prayed. But Paul says you can't hear Him or even know that He's there if He's not in you. Get the picture?

"Lord, I can't make it on what I have coming in." He will supply all your needs. Is there anything you *need* that you don't have? A need is something you can't do without, not something it would be uncomfortable or embarrassing to do without.

"Lord, I can't help who I fall in love with." Love is a choice, an act of your will. Not only can you help who you love, God expects you to. He expects you to be deliberate in your choice to love. He also expects you to love them with His love, not yours. His love is holy and honest and doesn't seek its own. He doesn't have a problem with you loving that man. But love him enough to honor his wife. Love him enough to confess that affair as sin and repent of it. Love him enough to give him back to his wife and put him in right relationship with God.

Prayer that is born from solitude can't lie to God. It won't lie to God. Now, you might wonder what to do if you haven't had time to seek solitude before you pray. Sometimes we need God right quick and in a hurry. "Help!" "Mercy!" "Save me!" "JESUS!!" Those prayers are always true. And if you pray them with an intense desire to be heard, God will hear you and rush to your side with peace to sustain you until your change comes.

Study is as important to your spiritual life as prayer and solitude. The study referred to here is not Monday night Bible study at your church. It's not you in a room with anywhere from ten to a few hundred people shouting and praising His holy name. There is a time and a place for that, but not in this part of this chapter. Silent, personal study of the Word of God should be a part of every spiritual devotion. When we give ourselves to examining the Scriptures and extracting the truth from them, we learn what is the perfect will of God concerning us. You should be a planted, committed member of a Spirit-filled, Bible-believing church. However, Sunday worship or midweek Bible study should complement your understanding of the Word, not comprise it.

When the man or woman of God preaches or teaches, God can speak through them and give you understanding as well as a "word" for your particular situation. Sooner or later, though, you need to grow up and learn how to get your own word. Pastor won't be there to tell you what "thus saith the Lord" while that brother is trying to feel up under your blouse. Your discipleship leader can't go to your job with you and protect you from all the back-biters and gossipmongers. You can't pop in the tape from last Sunday in the middle of an argument with your husband. David said he hid the Word of God in his heart to keep him from sin (see Ps. 119:11). What are you hiding in your heart? Somebody else's words? Somebody else's understanding? Somebody else's interpretation?

God did not say, "In the beginning were the 'words,' and the 'words' were with God, and the 'words' were God." He said, "In the beginning was the *Word*, and the *Word* was with God, and the *Word* was God" (Jn. 1:1). When you study, you're not looking for what the words say. You're looking for the Word that is the Way, the Truth and the Life. Pastor can't find that for you. Friends can't find that for you. Teachers can't defend that for you. We overcome satan by the "word of our testimony" (see Rev. 12:11). God will infuse your life with the truth of who He is in you. If you don't learn to recognize that truth, how do you expect to be able to use it to overcome satan? And what if, God forbid, you have to defend the truth against one of those pastors or teachers or friends? Could you? Or would the glory of God be extinguished in your ignorance? Solitude makes it possible to hear God. Prayer makes it possible for God to hear us. In study, we learn about this God that we seek to hear and who we want to hear us.

Did it ever occur to you that while you want to hear God, He wants to hear you? While you want God to hear you, He wants you to hear Him. Solitude and prayer expose our hearts to God as we bask in the truth. Study exposes God's heart to us in the same manner. Letting somebody else be your only source of knowledge is like letting somebody else chew your food for you. Do you really want to do that?

Solitude, prayer and *study*—these three protect the power we receive from God by continually cleansing our spirit of the debris of untruth that breeds sin. As we consistently and diligently give ourselves to each of them, every person, place, thing, habit or vain imagination that tries to clutter our hearts is brushed away. Our spirits are not self-cleaning organisms; they require constant attention and care. Fortunately, the Creator gives us power to keep things in order.

Now unto Him that is able to keep you from falling, and to present you faultless before the presence of His glory with exceeding joy, to the only wise God our Saviour, be glory and majesty, dominion and power, both now and for ever. Amen (Jude 24-25).

From My Heart

Mrs. Far Above Rubies (Proverbs 31:10-31)

She's a Good Woman
1. She works diligently: She *"worketh willingly with her hands"* (13, 15, 19).
2. She contrives prudently: She *"considereth...and buyeth"* (16, 22, 24).
3. She behaves uprightly: *"Strength and honour are her clothing"* (25).

She's a Good Wife
1. She seeks her husband's good: *"She will do him good...all the days of her life"* (12).
2. She keeps his confidence: *"The heart of her husband doth safely trust in her"* (11).
3. She aids his prosperity: *"Her husband is known...among the elders of the land"* (23-24).

She's a Good Mother
1. She clothes her family well: *"All her household are clothed with scarlet"* (21).
2. She feeds her family well: *"She riseth...and giveth meat to her household"* (15, 27).
3. She shops sensibly: *"She bringeth her food from afar"* (14, 18).

She's a Good Neighbor
1. She helps the poor: *"She stretcheth out her hand to the poor"* (20).
2. She uplifts the needy: *"She reacheth forth her hands to the needy"* (20).
3. She speaks graciously: *"In her tongue is the law of kindness"* (26).

Her Value: "Her price is far above rubies."
Her Praise: "Her children arise up, and call her blessed."
Her Preeminence: "But thou excellest them all."
Her secret: "A woman that feareth the Lord."

From Your Heart

Meditate on the following passages:

I am thy shield, and thy exceeding great reward...I will do a new thing; now it shall spring forth...thy Maker is thine husband; the Lord of hosts is His name...I have chosen you, and ordained you, that ye should go and bring forth fruit...I will pour My spirit upon thy seed, and My blessing upon thine offspring...and ye shall be witnesses unto Me...that light is come into the world...if ye abide in Me, and My words abide in you...ye are the light of the world...Let your light so shine before men, that they may see your good works, and glorify your Father which is in heaven.

1. Thank God for the areas in your life where His light shines brightest in you.

_____

_____

_____

2. Where is it difficult to see? What are the "dark" areas in you and around you?

_____

_____

_____

Chapter Four

Omniscience...
Omnipresence...Omnipotence

What do you do when you are fully aware that as a Christian woman, mother, friend, worker, minister, wife and sister, you should "study to be quiet," "love those that despitefully use you," and forgive the unforgivable—but instead find that you're angry, uptight, cantankerous, evil, mean, jealous, promiscuous, lazy, cruel, controlling, manipulative and boisterous? What do you do when you really want to walk in the Spirit but keep bumping into your flesh and its dictates? What do you do when you really want to walk by faith and not by sight, but you're so full of fear, worry and doubt that you don't know what to believe? What do you do when you know that you should love your enemies, but right now you can't stand the sight of your friends? What do you do when you discover that while you once were so financially blessed that you could lend to the poor, now you feel cursed because you can't even qualify for a loan yourself!

What do you do when you know you should be teaching other women to be sober, but you're silly, high and drunk? You should be telling other women to love their husbands, but instead you're telling them to walk out because you're not happy in your own marriage right now. You know that you should be teaching others to love, train and discipline their children, but you are aborting and abusing your children. What should you do when you should be telling other women to become "discreet, of sound mind, self-controlled, sober-minded," but you yourself have become wild, wayward and actually crazy with pain and heartache? How do you exhort other women to be chaste and celibate and yet you have "yielded your members servants to uncleanness and to iniquity"?

When do you seek help for yourself because, while you tell other women to become "keepers at home," you have become idle, with no purpose or destiny? "You wander from house to house, gossiping and tattling, a busybody speaking things which you ought not" (see 1 Tim. 5:13).

When we should be teaching younger women to marry, bear children, guide the house and give no occasion to the adversary, we have become so resentful and turned off to men and marriage that we seek the company of females for social and sometimes sexual pleasure. How do you explain that you know you're not a lesbian and you know you're not bisexual, but you're so hurt, so angry, so hostile and disgusted that you no longer wish for relationships with men, so you built walls to protect yourself from any and all men? How do you keep from allowing your own gall to poison the hearts of your daughters against men, or keep from turning your sons into the men you despise?

Bitterness—that acrid, lingering, troubling disease of the heart—is the greatest obstacle to realizing the fullness of God's power in us. Bitterness is that intense, distasteful and afflicting mixture of disappointment, anger, loneliness, fear and blame that causes us to weep when others rejoice and rejoice when others weep. Bitterness saps our moisture and smothers our hope. If we allow it to take root in us, it will choke the breath out of everything joyful, peaceful and life-producing in us. Bitterness will cause the sweet fragrance of true worship to become a stench in the nostrils of the Almighty. Most importantly, bitterness will rob us of the ability and the authority to recognize and reveal God. Bitterness, if it is not checked, will render us powerless in our marriages, in our ministries, in friendship, in caring for our children and in every spiritual discipline.

Bitterness is one of satan's most effective weapons against us because it makes us powerless from the inside out, so that by the time anyone sees bitterness in our behavior, its roots are already squeezing the life from our hearts. Moreover, it usually shows up as anger, pride, sarcasm, hostility—anything except what it is. So it alienates us from loved ones and cuts off other avenues of help when we are often too weak or unwilling to help ourselves. Once we find ourselves alone, satan uses our bitterness to turn us against God. We blame Him, so we stop praying and praising, cutting off the source of all our power, and therefore separating us from our deliverance.

Can we win over our bitterness? We can and we must, not just for our sakes, but for those around us. Hebrews 12:15 says many are defiled when we allow bitterness to "spring up" within us. You've seen that timid, hollow-eyed child walking on eggshells around his bitter mother. You know that nervous secretary with the bitter boss. You've felt the sting of that single girlfriend who snapped at you when you tried to tell her how sweet your husband was the other day. "Can we change the subject? Some of us ain't as 'blessed' as you are!" Bitter teachers kill a child's curiosity. Bitter preachers produce angry, jealous, covetous sheep. Bitter police are brutal, at home and on the job. Bitter politicians corrupt the system. Bitter doctors treat pocketbooks, not patients.

If we are to become women who walk in power, we must learn to recognize, overcome and protect ourselves from bitterness and every rancid fruit it produces. God is looking for vessels willing to receive and reproduce His power in their lives, in their homes, on their jobs and throughout the world. His word to us in these last days is to get rid of our bitterness. How do we do that? The same way you get rid of weeds in a garden. You don't just pull up what you can see. You have to dig up the roots. At the root of every bitter thing in our hearts is one of three lies that the enemy has told us about God: 1) He doesn't understand my problem. 2) He has left me to deal with it alone. 3) He can't do anything about my problem. The first lie makes us feel isolated. The second lie makes us feel forsaken. The third lie makes us feel hopeless. Together, they conspire to make us feel frustrated and angry with the promises of God, and that produces bitterness.

In reality, bitterness is an issue of unbelief. If we are believing lies, then there are obviously some truths we are *not* believing at the same time. To rid ourselves of bitterness, we have to embrace the truth that will obliterate the lie. 1) He does understand my problem, because *God is omniscient.* 2) He has not left me alone, because *God is omnipresent.* 3) He can fix my problem, because *God is omnipotent.* These three truths about God shine light on bitterness and keep it from contaminating our heart and cutting off our power.

God's Omniscience

To say that God "knows everything" is like saying motherhood is "feeding babies." It's true, but it doesn't really paint a complete picture. It barely scratches the surface. In First Samuel 2:3, Hannah says "the Lord is a God of knowledge." In the original Hebrew, knowledge is plural. In other words, the Lord is a God of "knowledges," meaning all kinds of knowledge. He knows what every living thing knows. He knows what angels know, what men know and what devils and demons know. He knows all that can be known *about* everything, living and not living, in the heavens and on earth. He lives in yesterday, today and forever. So, too, does His knowledge. He can tell you right now what you will be thinking tomorrow. And He knows, Himself, the one thing only He can know, because He is without end or beginning. The psalmist in Psalm 147:5 says, "His understanding is infinite."

God's knowledge is not simply a collection of data. He is as infinitely wise as He is knowledgeable. He knows what, where, why and how everything exists as itself and in relation to every other thing. He knows what can happen, what should happen and what will happen to, in, with, for and between all people, nations, creatures, plants, minerals, elements and objects in the entire universe. What God knows is impossible to say, because He also knows everything that is not known, not seen and not understood. As He is, God's knowledge is perfect. There is no margin of error, no question, no place for exception or caveat in His knowledge. He sees everything as it truly is, was and will be, and He has a complete understanding of everything that He sees. And He sees you.

He sees you and He sees your heart. He knows everything that you're going through. He knows the pain you feel because the man you married would rather be with someone else. He knows that the promotion you wanted so badly brought stress and high blood pressure with it. He knows and understands that you give your tithes and offerings every week and still drive a raggedy car and live in a one-bedroom apartment with your three fatherless children. He knows you sacrificed your dreams and desires for your husband and children, and yet that husband has left you for a younger, bolder, braver woman. You know it's wrong, but it destroys you to know that your children are crazy about their new stepmom. He knows you raised your kids to know and love Him. He knows you took two jobs to educate them in a private Christian school. And He knows how devastated you are to learn that your 17-year-old daughter is pregnant.

He knows all that you go through, and not because you prayed it. Some of your pain is so deep that you don't even know about it. He knows because He is concerned about you. While you think about your current situation and remember what you used to be, have, do, hope for and dream about, God wants you to know that He knew you before you were—before you had anything, did anything, hoped for or dreamed about anything. He knew you before you were born, and He loved you then. He knew you before that. He was the One supervising your growth and development in your mother's womb.

It's hard to imagine that a God who knows all things could see our bitterness and not understand that we have a right to it. But we don't have a right to it, because we don't know all things. So when the God who does know all tells us to hold on, we hold on, because if He knows our tomorrow, He must know there's a reason to hold on. When we don't understand why people are allowed to hurt us with seeming impunity, and our Father says forgive them, we do. After all, He said vengeance is His, so He must know how to punish evildoers and restore our reputation at the same time. Our Lord says He knows the plans He has for us. We may not understand why we feel such rejection at work. But He may be planning to promote us to a management position where we'll be required to encourage and motivate others. The rejection we're feeling now will help us then. You may not like having to watch every dime that comes into the house, stay on a tight budget or create new ways every month to make your money go further. But God may be planning to marry you to a man of God with a home-based business, and you may need to serve as his accountant until the business is a success (and God has already planned its success).

We all have plans. But God has plans too, and His plans include more than our time here on earth. His plans for us are eternal ones. We may need to wait, or suffer, or endure, so that we can become stronger and better able to escape the devourer. We may have to be strong enough to snatch somebody else out of his jaws.

Keep in mind that while God knows about everything that concerns us, we're not the only ones on this planet. He loves that bruised and broken sister who keeps lashing out at you. He knows why she's hurting, and His plans include her healing along with yours. He knows and cares about that father who treats his kids so badly. Watch him restore all of them without destroying any of them.

The Bible tells us that each person is unique—physically, emotionally and spiritually—and that God shaped the integral parts of us all. Psalm 139:1-3, 13-14 declares:

> *O Lord, Thou hast searched me, and known me. Thou knowest my downsitting and mine uprising, Thou understandest my thought afar off. Thou compassest my path and my lying down, and art acquainted with all my ways. ...Thou hast covered me in my mother's womb...I am fearfully and wonderfully made: marvelous are Thy works; and That my soul knoweth right well.*

Wives, are you aware that God did not write these verses just for you, but also for your husband? Yes, that grouchy but anointed man. Yes, that ornery but anointed man. Yes, that stubborn but anointed man. Yes, yes, yes, God wrote these verses not just for you, but for him. While He knows what you're going through and feeling, remember that He knows what your husband is going through and feeling too. Your purpose on this earth is wrapped up in His holy assignment. So if it seems like God doesn't know what's going on with you, it might be because He's trying to work some things out in your husband as well.

In his letter to the Galatians, the apostle Paul proclaims that even while he was in his mother's womb, God set him apart to preach to the Gentiles. God was aware of Paul's personality before his conversion. In fact, He helped develop it. He knew that Paul's particular behavioral style would be useful in completing his mission. "...God [set me apart] from my mother's womb, and called me by His grace, to reveal His Son in me, that I might preach Him among the [Gentiles]" (Gal. 1:15-16).

Paul was a creative, dominant individual, educated in the best schools, well connected politically and socially. He was well suited to proclaim the gospel to the Gentiles. God also had allowed him to be a consenting witness to the death of Stephen. He heard that first martyr of Christ cry out to God to forgive his murderers. Paul himself had persecuted Christians. What greater testimony could there be of God's grace? And who would be more believable as a witness than Paul, who had nothing to gain from his conversion and everything to lose? God knew that; before Paul was Saul and before Saul was anybody, God knew.

Do you ever wonder what God knows about you? When you find yourself tempted to embrace the bitterness that comes from feeling isolated, instead of asking yourself "Why?" ask "What?" "What is my omniscient Father trying to show me? What is He trying to tell me? What is He preparing me for? What will I use all of this patience for? What is He planning to do *for* me that requires Him to do this *to* me?" Even when all is well with you, ask God in your prayers what He knows about you. You'll find out that He knows all your secrets, all your dreams, all your fears, all your mistakes...and He knows that He loves you.

Once we understand that God knows all that we think, feel and experience, we can begin discern to His omniscience in us. Remember, woman of God, God has given you His Spirit. Although that doesn't mean you will know all things, it does mean that you have access to the wisdom of God to contend with confusion, expose lies and bring light to dark situations. When we suffer at the hands of others, God's wisdom in us can show us a broken, discouraged, abused heart that doesn't know how not to cause pain. When our husbands ignore us, God's Spirit can cut through the confusion we're feeling and possibly show us a man whose fear of intimacy causes him to reject us.

Jeremiah says the heart is wicked and deceitful. He asks, "Who can know it?" (see Jer. 17:9) God can. He knows the reason for our anger, jealousy, fear, unforgiveness, depression and insecurity. And He's willing to share His knowledge with us, if we will give up our right to our bitterness. The power of God's wisdom, understanding and knowledge is the power to know ourselves and others. It is also the power to know God's love and endure through the painful parts of it "for the joy set before us." It is the power to discern the hearts of men and the Word and will of God. It is the power to know, by faith, that we are watched, understood and cared for by One who never sleeps and whose eyes see everything around and in us.

God's Omnipresence

The popular view of God's omnipresence reveals Him as a God who is everywhere, all the time, at the same time. And that is true. Scripture attests to it:

> *But will God indeed dwell on the earth? behold, the heaven and heaven of heavens cannot contain Thee; how much less this house that I have builded?* (1 Kings 8:27)

> *Whither shall I go from Thy spirit? or whither shall I flee from Thy presence? If I ascend up into heaven, Thou art there: if I make my bed in hell, behold, Thou art there. If I take the wings of the morning, and dwell in the uttermost parts of the sea; even there shall Thy hand lead me, and Thy right hand shall hold me* (Psalm 139:7-10).

> *Can any hide himself in secret places that I shall not see him? saith the Lord. Do not I fill heaven and earth? saith the Lord* (Jeremiah 23:24).

> *Though they dig into hell, thence shall Mine hand take them; though they climb up to heaven, thence will I bring them down* (Amos 9:2).

God is in all places at all times. We can't go anywhere that He isn't. However, there is another perspective of the Lord's omnipresence that is more relevant as we consider this issue of bitterness and its effect on our ability to walk with power—one that takes into account that sometimes we get lonely. Sometimes, even in a crowd, we feel like we're by ourselves. Sometimes we feel shut off from the rest of the world, out of touch and out of step. At times like that it's hard to believe that our Father, who art in heaven, on earth and in a million places, doing a million things for a million people, has the time or the desire to check on us. Our own little individual corner of existence is just a speck next to a whole country, much less a world or the entire universe, for that matter.

When we get weighed down by stress, depression, anger, fatigue, confusion, hurt, disgust or numerous responsibilities and obligations, it doesn't always comfort us to know that God is moving, solving, healing or loving the whole world. We want His full attention. We want His whole heart, undivided. We want the full force of His grace, His mercy, His loving-kindness, His peace and His joy. That's when it's good to know that to say God is omnipresent doesn't just mean He stretches out to infinity. It also means God is "all-present," meaning He's always and in all ways "close to," "near to," "next to" and "right here with" me. In fact "omnipresent" literally means all or completely present, or here. It is true that God can go everywhere. But it is just as true that He is everywhere you go. Yes, God lives in yesterday, today and tomorrow. He also lives in *my* yesterday, today and tomorrow.

God wants us to have an understanding of His closeness to us. He sent His son Emanuel, "God with us," as an expression of that facet of His love. When Emanuel left the earth, like His Father, He sent someone, the Comforter, to be with us until His return.

Power is useless if it's not accessible. Our biggest challenge, in our lives, relationships, ministry and at work, is believing that God's power is available to us at any given moment, and, once believing, availing ourselves of it. But God's Word says He has not moved from you. He can't if He's in all places at all times. He is in front of you to lead you, beside you to protect you, behind you to encourage you, beneath you to support you and in you to counsel, comfort and constrain you. He's closer than your best friend who loves you but who is not with you always. He's closer than your husband, the one whose bone and flesh find their substance in you. He's closer to you than you are to yourself, for it is in Him that you live and move and have your very being (see Acts 17:28). There is not a cell in your body that does not know Him. Even as He directs the parts of your life that are visible to you, He is moving, shaping, reshaping, refining and defining you at a molecular level and beyond. Before any healing comes to your body in the natural, He has already done battle in the spirit realm to seal it.

Implicit in any understanding of the omnipresence of God is the notion of volition. God, knowing His own nature and composition, chose to make us. He knew we could have no life outside of Him. He knew we would live in Him and that He would certainly live in us. He made us because His desire is to be close to us. Don't let the enemy tell you the lie that you are alone and that nobody wants to be with you in your mess. God loved you, then made you knowing that you would have mess. He sent His only Son to die so that you would not have to be separated from Him. The omnipresence of God is one of the greatest illustrations of His love for mankind and His desire for intimacy with us. Who are we that He should care so much about us? We are His, made by Him for His pleasure.

With all this in mind, it seems impossible that we could ever be apart from God. Yet, it happens. We all have sensed the "absence of His presence" at one time or another. We prayed and cried, supplicated sorrowfully, energetically and importunately; pressed, pushed and pleaded in our closet, prostrate on the floor, in the shower, in the car, quietly quaking with fear, bold with arrogance, humiliated and broken. And still we could not hear, see or feel Him. So we begin to question Him. *Didn't You say You would never leave me or forsake me? Are You not my Shepherd? I thought You said nothing could separate me from You!* We ask, then accuse Him, thinking He betrayed us. But He hasn't. It's not possible for Him to lie anymore than it is possible for Him to leave us.

Through Jeremiah the Lord asks, "Am I a God at hand...and not a God afar off?" (Jer. 23:23) When we feel far from God, it's not because God somehow "moved away" from us. It's because of the dissimilarity of our natures. God is a Spirit who exists in all places at all times. He is also light, and light cannot have communion with darkness. Try this little experiment. Make your hand into a fist. If you were to find yourself inside that fist, it would certainly be dark there. Now, open your hand and release the darkness into the room. What happened? The dark is no more, because darkness cannot co-exist with light. When our hearts are "darkened" by unbelief, sin or a lack of understanding, it's as though our hearts exist inside that fist, separated from the light and unable to communicate with it. But when we walk as John says "in the light," we know the presence of God, because God is light (see 1 Jn. 10:5-7).

When we settle into our bitterness, convinced that God doesn't care about us or that He has left us alone, we're in darkness and are as "far" from God as darkness is from light. When we choose to live in sin, again we're in darkness. When we operate from a lack of understanding concerning the Word of God, we are in darkness. But if our heart cries out to God, putting us at the mercy of His grace, we have stepped out of darkness and into the light. And if we choose to put away the works of the flesh and set our affections on the things of the Spirit, we become the children of Light. When God is silent, and we know by faith that He hasn't left us or forsaken us, despite appearances, then we are walking in the light. At that point, as David puts it in Psalm 139:12, "the night shineth as the day: the darkness and the light are both alike...."

When we walk in the power of the presence of God, we begin to recognize His presence in all things. We know He's beside us in that board meeting, giving us wisdom and favor. We know He's in the gentle, loving way we talk to our husband. We feel Him behind us, giving us powerful words to preach to hungry, broken souls. We see Him leading us along as we change jobs, choose friends and search for deliverance from sin. We sense Him as the floor beneath us and as the sky over our heads. When we welcome Him in us, there is power to dodge the fiery darts of the enemy and the slings and arrows we've aimed at ourselves. Depression, jealousy and bitterness have no place to sit in the soul of a woman aware of the omnipresence of God. Only power resides in that temple.

God's Omnipotence

God has called us to be women of influence. We are women whom He has chosen and earmarked for prominence, power and

greatness, not to glorify and magnify our mundane, average existence, but to glorify and magnify His holy One. We are "died, fried
and laid to the side." We have "died" to sin, we've been "fried" in
the fires of trial and tribulation, and we were "laid to the side," or
set aside, distinguished as part of God's "firstfruits" offering to
Himself. There is a piece of God's light in you waiting to be
birthed into this dark world. There is healing balm dripping from
your fingertips to soothe the scarred and wounded soul. There is
a word sharpening itself in your spirit, ready to cut asunder every
lie and evil trick of the enemy. There is power in you, purposed
for release at God's appointed time, that will answer the desperate
cry of a captive man, woman, boy or girl. And there is power in
you that is available to you right now—put there to compel you to
yield to God's will for you, then to propel you into your destiny.

But some of you are struggling with the notion that God
wants to work miracles through you. Some of you are angry.
You've been faithful to God, obedient to His Word and yet...that
private, secret desire to marry has not been granted, and you're
almost 40 years old. Some of you know you can preach and teach,
but no one is calling you to speak at conferences or meetings and
pastor overlooks you at church Sunday after Sunday. Some of you
saved yourself for marriage only to find yourself—30 days after
your wedding—infected with a sexually transmitted disease, a "gift"
from your new husband. Some of you are looking at your lives and
you don't believe anything's brewing beneath the surface of your
pitiful 24-7-365. God surely didn't call you to anything other than
to be the poster child for the Hall of Shame.

Oh, but He did, sister. You see, we serve an omnipotent God,
a God who is perfect and holy in unlimited strength, might,
dominion, force and enforcement. Our God is awesome. He erect-
ed an entire universe with a thought, and He could level it all
tomorrow with another thought. Moses praised Him at the Red
Sea, singing, "...with the blast of Thy nostrils the waters were gathered together, the floods stood upright as an heap, and the depths
were congealed in the heart of the sea" (Ex. 15:8). God Himself
declares His raiment to be majesty, excellency, glory and beauty
(see Job 40:10). And when you declared Him to be your Lord, He
put some of that power in you with plans to use it.

It's easy to think that God has doled His strength out to some and not to others. How is it that one sister can run off 30 imps with one anointed rebuke and another screams at the devil all night long and doesn't upset anybody but the neighbors? How did one quiet preacher who spoke for ten minutes cause dozens to come weeping to the altar, while Rev. Hoop 'n' Holler Gimme a Dollar barely kept his people awake? How do you shake yourself from the bitterness and depression that makes you fall asleep whenever you try to pray? How do you silence the voice in your spirit that keeps telling you that you just don't have the anointing that other saint has? How do you look at the mistakes you've made, the times you "missed God," the disappointments and the heartaches, and not wonder if you're one of the "weak sheep"? Maybe you believe that God can do anything for you and through you, but you're just not sure He wants to.

God's omnipotence is not just found in His ability to do all things. It is also found in His attitude about all that He does. Omnipotence infuses every part of God's nature. His sense of justice is a powerful one. His holiness is unlimited in its essence. There is no part of God's nature that is not saturated with every other part. So then, His love for you can't be separated from His infinitude, His grace, His mercy, His omniscience, His omnipresence or His omnipotence. In other words, when God says He cares about you, He's not talking about some casual holy fling. He is deeply, passionately, powerfully in love with you! When He says you are the temple of the Holy Spirit, His Spirit, He has declared His intent to make you capable of housing the strongest force in the universe. And when He says He wants to give you the desires of your heart, He's going to give them to you as only He can.

Be careful what you ask for from an omnipotent God. He's not going to give you just any husband. You'd better get ready for a demon-slaying, praying, anointed, affectionate, Spirit-filled king! Did you ask for a child who loves the Lord? Don't be surprised if the doctor smacks him on the behind, and he turns around and lays his chubby hands on the doctor and heals him before he lets out a cry. You're looking for wisdom? You might get Solomon's. An omnipotent God doesn't just give knowledge, success and health. He gives prophetic gifts, exceeding abundance and eternal life. Do you know who He is? Do you know who you are to Him?

When we get a true understanding of the omnipotence of God in our spirits, we have the power to move into our destiny. The greatest enemy of our destiny is our history. What we used to be, used to want, used to have and used to do can imprison us in bitterness, discontentment and disappointment, making it impossible to "press forward unto those things that are before us" (see Phil. 3:13-14). But where there is bitterness, discontentment and disappointment, there was once expectation, contentment and hope. There were some things we once desired and hoped for. Time, trial and temptation can turn our dreaming into discouragement if we don't comprehend or believe in the omnipotent ability, wisdom and love of God. He can give us the desires of our hearts. He wants to. But only He knows when and how we should have them.

When we operate in the power of our omnipotent Lord, we don't just minister. We pull up, tear down, bind and loose. We don't just pray; we bow down in complete worship. We don't just win; we are "more than conquerors." We have unlimited power to let go of yesterday's disappointments and welcome contentment as we let our faith carry us into tomorrow.

God has called you to be a woman of influence. So if you must, you have the power to encourage yourself. You have the power to see your purpose, recognize your anointing and look forward to your destiny. When Samson's mother birthed him, a child born to destroy the enemies of Israel, the Bible says she named him Samson (which means "like the sun"). It says, "and the child grew, and the Lord blessed him. And the Spirit of the Lord began to move him..." (Judg. 13:24-25). These are the three ingredients of anointing. When you are anointed, God grows you, blesses you and moves you. You have the Spirit of the Lord. God will grow you. He will bless you. And His Spirit will begin to move you toward becoming the woman He decided you would be before He made the earth and suspended it in space.

When you discern God's omnipotence in yourself, in others and in the things around you, you can take everything the enemy throws at you. You won't become alarmed if in your life you become damaged, devastated or cast to the side. Remember, people look at broken things and call them junk. God looks at all things *not* broken and calls them useless. Every trial is His invitation to you to grow. Every setback is a setup for you to be blessed beyond your expectations. The woman with the issue of blood was looking for a healing. What she received was the power to be made whole.

Look at those hands again. Are you sure there's no healing power in them? Check your spirit. There might be a word or two in there. And that's definitely light shining in and through you.

> *And I heard as it were the voice of a great multitude, and as the voice of many waters, and as the voice of mighty thunderings, saying, Alleluia: for the Lord God omnipotent reigneth* (Revelation 19:6).

Hallelujah, indeed. He's reigning in you!

From My Heart

Can We Win Over Bitterness?

Can we find relief and deliverance from the overpowering spirit of bitterness; the evil that cripples us, blocks us and stops us from becoming the great, gracious, wonderful, exciting women and ladies God wants us to become? God never asks anything of us that He will not equip us to do. In Ephesians 4:31-32 we find His will concerning this sin.

Let all bitterness, and wrath, and anger, and clamour, and evil speaking, be put away from you, with all malice: and be ye kind one to another, tenderhearted, forgiving one another, even as God for Christ's sake hath forgiven you.

Regardless of what happens to you, make up your mind to overcome bitterness. God says be aggressive about eliminating it from your heart. Here's how:

1. Admit that you're living with bitterness. Confess it like any other sin (see 1 Jn. 1:9).
2. Ask God to show you how it's damaging you (see Prov. 16:2).
3. Admit that it is your issue, no one else's (see Mt. 7:5).
4. Stop nursing and rehearsing your bitterness with others (see Mt. 15:11).
5. Stay in harmony with godly friends and associates (see Prov. 11:14).
6. Soak your soul in the truth of the Scriptures (see Mt. 13:18-23).
7. Plan new experiences for your future. Think ahead, not backwards (see Phil. 3:13-14).
8. Be filled with the Spirit, for then bitterness can be "choked" out of you (see Gal. 5:16).
9. Study winners in the Bible who chose contentment over bitterness (see Gen. 50:20).
10. Finally, know that winning over bitterness—when you make up your mind—is just a matter of time, *but it will take time* (see Rom. 8:25-30).

From Your Heart

Meditate on each segment of the following passages:

O clap your hands, all ye people...He hath put a new song in my mouth, even praise unto our God...Who laid the foundations of the earth, that it should not be removed for ever...how manifold are Thy works! in wisdom hast Thou made them all: the earth is full of Thy riches...Thou art very great...All the paths of the Lord are mercy and truth...The heavens declare the glory of God...The Lord reigneth; let the earth rejoice...Who is this King of glory? The Lord of hosts, He is the King of glory...Praise, O ye servants of the Lord...I will bless the Lord at all times...Bless the Lord, O my soul.

Magnify the Lord and exalt His name in your own words:

Chapter Five

Word... Works... Worship

Can God trust you with power? Can He be sure that every gift He has given to you as preacher, wife, worker, mother, sister and friend will be used to His glory and not your own? Can you be sure that your zeal to serve God will not overshadow your meekness or dull your spiritual senses? You can if you understand and operate according to the currency and current of the Kingdom of God.

Every country, government or kingdom has an economy, a system for the management of resources and production of goods and services, as well as a currency, or money in circulation as a medium of exchange. Our economy uses the dollar as our unit of currency. Germany has the deutsche mark, Greece the drachma, Israel the shekel. All over the world, those considered to be the wealthiest people are the ones who have or have access to the most currency. Now, that concept did not begin with the world. God is the Lord of all wealth. He alone gives us power to get wealth (see 1 Sam. 2:7-8; Deut. 8:18), because all worldly wealth belongs to Him (see Ps. 24:1).

God's Kingdom also operates by an economy. As citizens of the Kingdom, "our system for the management of resources and production of goods and services" is the Word of God. We give and receive "goods and services" in the Kingdom according to that economy. Now, the currency—the "money" used as the medium of

exchange—in God's Kingdom is love. The economy of the Kingdom of God is different from that of the world because those who
would be "wealthy" don't try to accumulate the most currency.
They try to give the most away. In other words, the "rich kids" in
Christendom are the ones with the most love to give. In the world,
money is power. In the Spirit realm, love is power. The same God
who has and is all power, is the same God who says in First John
4:8 that He is love.

A "current" is a flow of electric charge, or power. In the
world, money or access to it brings power, so ambition, pride and
greed often control the flow of power in an economy. In the Kingdom, because love is the currency, humility is the current or the
conductor of power. Since love requires us to seek the wealth of
others before our own (see 1 Cor. 10:24), it cannot be accessed,
transmitted or transferred by pride, greed or ambition. The apostle Peter exhorts us to "humble yourselves therefore under the
mighty hand of God, that He may exalt you in due time" (1 Pet.
5:6). James says, "Humble yourself in the sight of the Lord, and He
shall lift you up" (4:10). God's power moves to and through us best
when our hearts are humble. We become rich in His love, which is
His power, when we walk in humility.

How does God know He can trust us with His power? He can
see the humility in you. How do *you* know He can trust you with
His power? You seek to humble yourself in your own eyes, in the
eyes of others and in the sight of God. You humble yourself in
your own eyes by devoting yourself to *living the Word of God*. You
humble yourself in the sight of others by devoting yourself to *doing
the works of God*. You humble yourself in the sight of God by devoting yourself to *becoming the worship of God*.

God gives us His power progressively, which means He gives
us more as we demonstrate that we can handle more. The Bible
says that when we are faithful over a little, He gives us much (see
Lk. 19:17). When we devote ourselves to the Word, the works and
the worship of God, His power can move in us, through us and for
us. And as we operate in the power we have, we increase our
capacity to harness, hold and release more of it.

Living Word

There is a war going on. The stakes are high, for we ourselves
are the spoils, and the enemy doesn't plan to take prisoners. He

wants us eliminated. His goal is to make us paupers in God's Kingdom, without power and therefore without the love of God and eternal life. But this is a strange fight that we're in. No one is grabbing a gun and jumping on a plane bound for some remote country filled with smoke and fatalities. We're not hearing about this war on the news (not explicitly, anyway). We can't see the enemy with our eyes, but we know he's there. We know his tactics. We recognize his signature on a situation or circumstance.

Paul says this enemy that we're supposed to be strong against, is comprised of "principalities, powers, rulers of the darkness of this world, and spiritual wickedness" (see Eph. 6:12). The strangest thing of all is that the battleground and the actual fighting are going on in two separate locations. The actual fighting is taking place in the spirit realm, but the battleground is the mind of each believer. We know this because Paul tells us in Second Corinthians 10:5 that the goal of our combat is the "casting down [of] imaginations, and every high thing that exalteth itself against the knowledge of God, and bringing into captivity [those thoughts] to the obedience of Christ." If satan can control our minds, he will win the war against us. He won't even have to drag us to our destruction. We'll gladly go, choosing any one of a million sinful paths, all designed to validate, reward and praise us for rejecting God. We will die merrily, perishing in the desert of our own pride and ignorance, or suffocate in a tomb of helpless self-deprecation or hopeless emotional desolation.

It seems like an impossible war to fight at times. First Lady, how do you keep from allowing thoughts about your husband's past infidelity haunt you every time he goes out of town? Daughter, how do you keep the painful remembrances of your mother's criticism from undermining your confidence as a mother? Sister, are you afraid everyone you meet thinks you're as ugly as *you* think you are? Ms. Senior Vice President, do thoughts that you're not smart enough, not tough enough, not young enough, not respected enough or not aggressive enough make you feel powerless in the privacy of your own heart? When that brother didn't call you like he said he would, woman of God, did you replay those songs in your head that go something like, "There must be something wrong with you. You're getting old, girl. Better lower your standards, or you may never find love. He doesn't have to be saved. He doesn't have to be a praying brother. You'll pray for both of you."

Thoughts can make us powerless because we act on what we think. If we give in to sinful thoughts, we will sin. That's right, we always think about sin before we commit it. You fantasize about an affair before you have it. You weigh the pros and cons and the chances of getting caught before you cheat on your taxes. You chose your words carefully before you cut your husband to pieces about his sorry lovemaking, his measly paycheck, his weak character or his woeful affections toward you. You've heard people say, "I didn't think first. I just did it." Maybe you've said it yourself. But that is a lie from the pit. Thought always precedes action. Every action and reaction begins as an impulse in the brain. Free will, by definition, means the "freedom to do what I will," and you can't exercise your will without exercising your thoughts. God was not so sloppy in His construction of man that He gave us free will and no control over it. That control is His Word.

God never intended for us not to have a sinful, ugly, angry, bitter or wicked thought. These things come to us naturally, courtesy of our fruit-eating ancestors Adam and Eve. Sin is their legacy to us. But we have a sword with which to fight every sin that threatens our relationship with God and hinders us from walking in the fullness of His power. The Word of God is listed among our armor in Ephesians 6:13-17. When we make the Word the standard by which we live, we make a conscious decision to humble ourselves before it and allow it to make all our decisions for us. We may think about cheating on our taxes, but when we see that "a false balance is abomination to the Lord: but a just weight is His delight" (Prov. 11:1) and humbly submit to that standard, we have defeated the devil and handled our power in a way that pleases God.

That godly mother and father may not be ready to be godly grandparents. They may not think they're ready to handle all the condemnation from their friends and their church because their 14-year-old daughter is pregnant. He is an elder. She heads the women's discipleship ministry. The town they live in is small, but the mouths are big. And their daughter doesn't even want the child. She's sorry. She's learned her lesson. A quiet, out-of-town abortion solves everybody's problem, doesn't it? But God's Word says He chose us "in Him" before the foundation of the world (see Eph. 1:4). We were alive to Him then. Before He formed us in our mothers' womb, He "knew" us (see Jer. 1:5). He sanctified us before we came forth from the womb. He called, glorified, justified and even named us before He said "Let there be light." And all over the world, people are fighting for the "right" to snatch beloved, called, sanctified, justified, glorified, predestinated souls out of God's hand because it would be inconvenient or humiliating to raise them. But those of us who know God can't allow the cares of the world to override the Word of God, which is our standard for living.

Paul tells us that we war against satan by bringing down every thought that exalts itself against a knowledge of God and bringing those thoughts into captivity to the obedience of Christ, who is the Word. That's a two-step process. First we cast down, or demolish, any thought that tries to exist in our minds as truth if it is in conflict with what we know to be true about God. If you're not sure whether or not what you're thinking, feeling, imagining or considering is consistent with who God is, find out. Ignorance is only blissful until it delivers us into the hand of satan and separates us from God. There are some things you won't have to pray about if you study the Word. There are some things God won't warn you about if you've ignored too many opportunities to see it in His Word. When the prodigal son asked for his inheritance and left home, his father did not stop him. He just rejoiced when he returned home. But everybody who leaves home doesn't make it back. Are you willing to take that risk? We often hear people say, "What I don't know can't hurt me." But in reality, sometimes what we don't know can kill us!

Secondly, we have to take our cast-down thoughts captive to the obedience of Christ, or the Word. What does that mean? It means we put the thought next to the Word that applies to it. Then we obey the Word whenever that thought enters our mind. When we want to holler back at our boss, we put that thought next to Proverbs 15:1 and take our thought captive by lining our behavior up with it: "A soft answer turneth away wrath: but grievous words stir up anger." We want to holler, but we know God would be pleased with a soft answer, so that's what comes out of our mouth. Our thoughts may precede our behavior, but our behavior doesn't always have to submit to our thoughts. That is the spiritual fruit of self-control.

Living by the Word means casting down every thought that attempts to rob you of your power in Christ. "I can't," "I'll never understand this," "God doesn't care about me," "God must be mad at me," "I'm a failure," "God won't forgive me," "I'm sorry, I couldn't help it; God's just going to have to forgive me later," are all thoughts that exalt themselves against your knowledge of God. The Word says you can do all things. You can ask for wisdom. A nursing mother would forget her child before God would forget you. He's faithful to forgive. But God is not mocked; you will reap what you sow—and the way some of us are sowing, we need to be praying for crop failure. Whenever you put your thoughts next to Scripture and there's a conflict, cast down the thought immediately. Refuse to honor it with corresponding sinful behavior. Assume your thoughts are wrong (because they are) and decide to let your behavior reflect the Scripture. That is the purest act of faith. When we believe God's Word over our own thoughts, we please God. Then God honors our faith by showing us in some way that we did the right thing.

Doing the Works

The Word you believe is seen in the works that flow from it. Faith may be the evidence of things not seen, but faith itself is definitely visible. Jesus said that when the Word of God is sown in "good ground," a person hears the Word, receives it and brings forth fruit, some thirtyfold, some sixty, and some a hundred. Fruit is visible, and it is produced to feed and nourish the hungry. Trees don't bear fruit to feed themselves. God put you here to help somebody, guide somebody, love somebody or grow somebody. When God created fruit, He declared that it would be a plant "whose seed is in itself" (Gen. 1:11). When the Word that is planted in you bears fruit through good works, you plant a seed in the heart and mind of every person you come in contact with. Look at Second Corinthians 3:1-3.

> Do we begin again to commend ourselves? or need we, as some others, epistles of commendation to you, or letters of commendation from you? Ye are our epistle written in our hearts, known

and read of all men: forasmuch as ye are manifestly declared to be the epistle of Christ ministered by us, written not with ink, but with the Spirit of the living God; not in tables of stone, but in flesh tables of the heart.

Paul humbled himself to do the work of God in the lives of the believers in Corinth, and that work became visible in their lives. Notice that Paul says the Corinthians were living epistles of Christ, ministered by them and written by the Spirit. In other words, their lives were a witness to Christ, and that witness was made visible by the Holy Spirit as Paul ministered, or served them. We don't create fruit. We bear it on our branches. We don't write the epistles that others become. Can the pen boast in a great sonnet that is written, or in the brilliant color of the ink on the page or the beauty of the penmanship? When we see the work God has done through us in the lives of others, we have nothing to do but be grateful that we were allowed to watch the "ink" flow through us.

As women behind the power, we are called and anointed to devote ourselves to being available for use by God through the Holy Spirit in the world. Ephesians 2:10 says we were made to do good works that were already on God's Day Planner for us to do. God planned that you would be powerful. He planned to move through you before you were born. In fact, He daily places you in a position to be powerful if you would humble yourself under His hand and submit to the works He has for you to do. Every opportunity to be kind is an opportunity to practice power. Every privilege to give, serve or help means another release of God's power through you. And every time God's power moves through you, you prove that you're ready to handle more of it.

A life without works is a life without power. James says faith without works is like a body without breath (see Jas. 2:26). So when we read Hebrews 11 and the lives of the heroes of faith are poured out before us, we can conclude that it is as much a testimony of works as it is faith. Jacob, Barak, Moses, Gideon, David, Samuel and others subdued kingdoms, "stopped the mouths of lions, quenched the violence of fire, escaped the edge of the sword, out of weakness were made strong." They endured trials, mocking, imprisonment, torture, poverty and persecution. Their faith was apparent in what they did, not in what they said they believed.

James gives us four portraits—two positive and two negative—of works and their importance in the Kingdom of God:

1. "Dead Man Walking"

If a brother or sister be naked, and destitute of daily food, and one of you say unto them, Depart in peace, be ye warmed and filled; notwithstanding ye give them not those things which are needful to the body; what doth it profit? Even so faith, if it hath not works, is dead, being alone (James 2:15-17).

How many times have you seen someone in need and just "whispered a word of prayer" instead of actually asking if there was anything you could do? Or if you did speak, you merely offered them a word of encouragement and sent them on their way? When we do the works that our faith in the Word directs us to, we become "walking word" versus "talking word." God does not put us in front of hurting and hopeless people for our entertainment. If He shows us a need and then shows us that we have the resources, time or talent to address that need, that's as good as His command for us to take care of it. Your desire to see a problem solved isn't worth much to the person with the problem. And your refusal to take active steps to help declares God a liar. He is a very present help. When you're present and able to help and you don't, you've wasted an opportunity to reveal a piece of God to somebody. That means you could have but didn't exercise your power.

The Word says the one who won't exercise his or her power when given the opportunity is as good as dead. Jesus called the Pharisees "whited sepulchers full of dead men's bones" (see Mt. 23:27). He said they looked pristine on the outside, but they were good-looking tombs. There was no life in them. Do you know any "whited sepulchers"? Folks raising hallelujah and hell at the same time? Passing out bulletins and fans on Sunday and the latest gossip the rest of the week? You've seen Sister Sepulcher, staying after church service to pray for that poor widow who lost her job, can't feed her kids and is living in her car. She's asking God to "send a miracle," but she owns an apartment building and has a few hundred dollars in the bottom of her $1,200.00 purse. She is the miracle, but she'd rather be a sideshow for all the people in the parking lot watching her "powerful" prayer.

2. "Profession vs. Possession"

Yea, a man may say, Thou hast faith, and I have works: show me thy faith without thy works, and I will show thee my faith by my works. Thou believest that there is one God; thou doest well: the devils also believe, and tremble (James 2:18-19).

The devil doesn't mind your believing in God as long as you don't act like you do. He knows that if you're content to let your relationship with God be a professed one and not a possessed one, no one will be able to tell you apart from the world, so you're not likely to lead anybody to Christ. You won't be a witness. You won't bear any fruit. He won't even have to waste his energy chasing you because, sooner or later, God—always true to His Word—will cut you off and toss you away (see Jn. 15:2). Then the devil—always true to his nature—will go about the business of destroying you (see 1 Pet. 5:8).

Works are not an option. You can't just choose not to do them and assume that your faith alone will save you. Through works we learn to trust and know God, and ultimately we become perfected by God. Our desire, our ability and our availability to do good works is our only proof that we are growing in God. If our faith doesn't move beyond our initial confession that "Jesus is Christ" to conduct that affirms and confirms that Christ is Lord of our life, the Bible says we're only about as holy as the average demon. They believe, and tremble. Some of us believe and can't even be bothered to fear the very God we say we know.

Profession without possession—that is, faith without works—is possibly the cruelest thing we can do to Jesus, because we assert our worthiness to wed Him in Heaven while alleging Him unworthy to be served on earth. We deny the power of His life and reduce the testimony of His death and resurrection to little more than a good story.

3. "Backdoor Blessing"

Likewise also was not Rahab the harlot justified by works, when she had received the messengers, and had sent them out another way? (James 2:25)

Rahab had probably never met God on a mountaintop. She wasn't with the burning bush crowd, or the Jordan-crossing, manna-eating, water-from-a-rock-drinking crew. But the Bible says she had heard about Joshua, and Moses before him. She knew about Egypt and the Red Sea. She knew the Lord was with them and that He had made them some promises, promises that included the city she lived in. Her own king had sent word to her to send the spies to him. She probably would have been paid very well for betraying them. But she hid them. She made them safe. And she made a deal with them...for her life.

Most of us haven't been to the mountaintop. Most of us don't dally around burning bushes, dine on manna or fill our water glasses from rock faucets. But most of us have heard about Joshua, and Moses before him. We've also heard about Jesus. He came knocking on our door one day, and we let Him in. But the prince of this world sends word to us every day to betray Him, to send Him out of our "house" so he can kill Him. If we believe Jesus is who He says He is, we know that the world can't offer us enough to compare to what Jesus is offering.

Rahab hid the spies. God wants us to hide His Son, the Word, in our hearts. Rahab's work saved her life. We can save ours too. When Joshua and the children of Israel destroyed Jericho, Rahab was the only one left standing. When we hide the Word in our hearts and protect the testimony of the Lamb by our works, everything around us may crumble, but we will be left standing. When this earth passes away, we will move on to eternal life.

Rahab's was a "backdoor blessing." You might not look like a candidate for the favor of God. People may have already counted you out. They may have decided that you won't amount to much. They may not know that you let Jesus in when they weren't looking. While they're talking about you behind your back, you're talking to Jesus. They don't invite you to lunch, but they don't know that you fill yourself every day with bread of life and living water. They see your bus pass and those same two dresses you wear to church every other Sunday, but they don't see the "Holy Ghost hope chest" God has given to you. In it is a white linen gown, a veil of purity, and a crown. And one day, while you're still on this earth, in due season, God will exalt you before them all. He'll give you every desire of your heart. He will bless you for your faithfulness to Him.

4. "Believing Is Seeing"

Was not Abraham our father justified by works, when he had offered Isaac his son upon the altar? Seest thou how faith wrought with his works, and by works was faith made perfect? And the scripture was fulfilled which saith, Abraham believed God, and it was imputed unto him for righteousness: and he was called the Friend of God (James 2:21-23).

Abraham believed God. The Scripture doesn't say Abraham believed *in* God. It doesn't say he believed *that* God would do this or that. It doesn't say he believed *what* God said or *who* God proclaimed Himself to be. Abraham believed God. Take a minute to really consider this. Look to God right now and make the following statements to Him, pausing between each to consider what you're actually saying:

"I believe in You, God."
"I believe that You care for me, God."
"I believe what You say, God."

It's not quite the same as saying, "I believe God." Most of us don't grow to the place of believing God. Many of us struggle to believe what we know about Him. To believe Him, you have to know Him. You have to seek to become His friend. Friends know what they can count on each other for. Friends protect and defend each other. Wife, you wouldn't let somebody run your husband down, would you? Friends vouch for each other's character. Friends enjoy one another's company. Friends give themselves to each other. Friends act like friends.

Are you friends with God yet? It's what He desires, you know. Sure, He's willing to be your Protector, Healer, Comforter, Father, Righteousness, Peace, Provider and even your Light in dark places. But what He wants most is to be your Friend and for you to become His. When you believe Him, no matter what things look like, you're God's friend. When you are willing to give up even the things He clearly gave to you, for His sake, you're His friend. When you stand firmly on His promises in the face of every devil, doubter and "discourager," you are His friend.

Jesus sat teaching in the temple one day and somebody interrupted Him to tell Him that His mother and brothers were waiting for Him outside. "And He answered them, saying, Who is My mother, or My brethren? And He looked round about on them which sat about Him, and said, Behold My mother and My brethren! For whosoever shall do the will of God, the same is My brother, and My sister, and mother" (Mk. 3:33-35). What are you doing to prove your relationship with God? Will Jesus stop you at the gates of Heaven and say, "Depart, I know you not"?

Go back to Genesis 22:1-19 and read the story of Abraham and his willingness to sacrifice Isaac. This is the passage where we first see the name Jehovah-jireh. We claim God as provider because we saw how He provided the ram in the bush for Abraham. However, Jehovah-jireh also means "the Lord will *see*." Yes, God did provide for Abraham on that mountain, and He provides for us every day. But look at verse 12. There God says, "...now I know that thou fearest God, seeing thou has not withheld thy son, thine only son from Me." God *saw* Abraham's faith through his actions. The place was named Jehovah-jireh because Jehovah "provided" *and* because Jehovah "saw."

Are you believing Jehovah-jireh for some things? What are you doing so that He can "know" or experience your belief? Maybe you are believing God for marriage one day. If He asked you to, would you be willing to give up that boyfriend you have? Perhaps you're waiting on that house God promised. Are you giving Him His tithe or are you putting it into the "down payment kitty"? You believe God is going to make you a preacher. Would you be willing to put that off indefinitely to serve your husband and children?

James says that Abraham believed God, and that his faith "was made perfect" by his works. When we act on what we believe, then, and only then, is our act of faith complete. How it must have pained Abraham to draw back that knife to slay his only son. Remember, he had just sent Ishmael away. God had promised to make Him a nation through Isaac. What would he tell Sarah when he got home? Moreover, here Isaac was a grown man watching his own father about to kill him. (Isaac's amazing faith is another story for another time.) We concern ourselves with all these issues. Abraham just did what his Friend asked him to do, knowing that He was more than able to ease every burden, defend every action and keep every promise concerning him. Abraham was willing to do his part and leave the rest of it up to God. Are we?

Becoming Worship

Historically, God shows Himself most powerful in the midst of our worship. When His people come, individually or corporately, and offer the sacrifice of their praise, thanksgiving, blessings and honor, something miraculous happens. There is no separation between God and man in true, Spirit-led worship. There is only glory given and received. The key to true worship is completeness. If anything is held back from God by the one worshiping, it is a statement to God that He is undeserving of it. As long as that lie is allowed to exist, "true" worship remains unattained and unattainable.

Israel often was accused of fulfilling the "act" of worship while falling short of actual worship. They offered the right animals, said the right words, performed the right tasks, but God was not pleased, for their hearts weren't in it. They didn't worship God; they worshiped to be seen as "godly," and God knew it. Oh, but when true worship took place, it was a sight to behold! Then God's glory became visible, tangible, sometimes audible and always powerful.

Today we're not required to sacrifice bulls, sheep and birds to meet our requirement of worship as the people of God. It might be easier if we were. Paul says we ourselves are the sacrifice God wants.

> *I beseech you therefore, brethren, by the mercies of God, that ye present your bodies a living sacrifice, holy, acceptable unto God, which is your reasonable service* (Romans 12:1).

Look at the New Living Translation:

> *And so, dear brothers and sisters, I plead with you to give your bodies to God. Let them be a living and holy sacrifice—the kind He will accept. When you think of what He has done for you, is this too much to ask?*

Is "everything" too much to ask? Well, God did require Jesus to give everything for us while we were still enemies with Him (see Rom. 5:6-8). How much more should we give Him back of ourselves? The amazing thing about worship is that while God requires it, He doesn't actually need it. He's no more God because you or I shout hallelujah. He's no weaker if we don't praise His strength. He's no less glorious because we didn't give Him His much-deserved glory. God is God all by Himself, so if you've got any ideas about Him needing your worship, go back a few pages and cast down that vain imagination.

When we worship God, we do it because He's worthy and we love Him. We are reverencing Him as Lord and basking in the fact of our relationship with Him. Sometimes our worship is simply our humble expression of our love for Him. Stevie Wonder recorded a song some years ago titled "I Just Called To Say 'I Love You.'" That's worship. That may seem trivial until you consider that our power is directly related to our willingness to worship Him, because power is the ability to recognize and reveal Him. Worship ushers us into the Lord's presence (God recognized). And when our lives acknowledge Him as Lord, He shows Himself through us to others (God revealed).

Worship is not for those who just want to wade into relationship with God. Devoting yourself to worship means totally submerging yourself in Him, dwelling in Him and running hard after the deepest part of His heart. Author Tommy Tenney calls it "God chasing." He says, "If you're a God chaser, you won't be happy to simply follow God's tracks. You will follow them *until you apprehend His presence.*"[1] That's the goal of worship: to "catch" God with your body, mind and spirit.

Paul beseeches us to present our person to God as a living sacrifice. In other words, we are to "become worship." Understand this. You've got to get up on the altar, die and let the fire of our holy Father consume you. Your life, lived in the beauty of holiness, is the sweet fragrance He longs to take into His nostrils. You are the gift He desires. "Know ye not that you are the temple of the Holy Spirit?" Your heart is His holy of holies. You house the Spirit of the living God, the same God who levels mountains and splits cedars. He lives in you. And when you worship Him with your time, your talent, your desires, your possessions, your thoughts,

---

1.   Tommy Tenney, *The God Chasers* (Shippensburg, PA: Destiny Image, 1998), p. xv.

your relationships and your devotion to Him, He is powerfully seen in you.

The model of worship is clear throughout Scripture, particularly in the Old Testament. If we look at the way offerings and sacrifices were handled by devout worshipers there, we're better able to understand what's expected of each of us as a living sacrifice. One of the most marvelous episodes of true worship occurs in First Kings chapter 18. There we find the prophet Elijah in his famous showdown against the 450 prophets of Baal at Mount Carmel. Elijah, whose very name means "my God is Jehovah," reflects his character as a man totally dedicated to God. That's why God was able to move so powerfully with him. Every miracle performed by God through Elijah challenged God's people to decide for or against God, and to bow or not bow accordingly. Elijah was worship walking daily. It's no surprise then that his most public act of worship is where we find the pattern of worship for our own lives.

> *And Elijah said unto all the people, Come near unto me. And all the people came near unto him. And he repaired the altar of the Lord that was broken down. And Elijah took twelve stones, according to the number of the tribes of the sons of Jacob, unto whom the word of the Lord came, saying, Israel shall be thy name: and with the stones he built an altar in the name of the Lord: and he made a trench about the altar, as great as would contain two measures of seed. And he put the wood in order, and cut the bullock in pieces, and laid him on the wood, and said, Fill four barrels with water, and pour it on the burnt sacrifice, and on the wood. And he said, Do it the second time. And they did it the second time. And he said, Do it the third time. And they did it the third time. And the water ran round about the altar; and he filled the trench also with water* (1 Kings 18:30-35).

The first thing Elijah did was *call the people near to him* so they could see what he was about to do. If you are to be a living sacrifice, know that God is going to put you in the spotlight. He wants to show you off. You may feel exposed, embarrassed and put on display, but that's how God is going to get the most glory from you as living worship. Don't avoid the publicity. Don't be surprised that your name is on everybody's lips. You may want to hide in your shame, but God is not going to let you. You need to know that as long as you're out there for everybody to see, *you are in the light*, and that means two things: 1) God has control of the situation, since He only gave satan dominion over darkness, and 2) God is about to heal, deliver, fix, exalt, restore, renew or help you right in the presence of your enemies. Psalm 23 says you are to fear no evil when you walk through the valley of the shadow of death. Those hurtful words are only shadows. Your desolation is only a shadow. Your pain is only a shadow. Always remember that where there are shadows, there is light. Walk in the light.

Next, Elijah *repaired the altar of the Lord that was broken down*. The altar is what holds or supports the sacrifice. It's what the sacrifice sits on. Everything that "defines" you is a part of your altar. Your job is a part of your altar, as are your family, your ministry, your finances, your marriage, your possessions, your talent, your health and your home. It's anything you see as part of the answer to the question, "Who are you?"

Our altars fall into disrepair over time if we neglect them or mismanage them. If you are so busy with ministry or work that your children suffer, or your husband feels "left," then your altar is "broken down." If you're still smoking or eating fat-filled foods after the doctor told you about your hypertension, your altar is damaged. Depression is often a symptom that the altar of your life is falling apart. God gave specific instructions in Exodus on how the altar was to be built for the Tabernacle of Moses. He's no less particular about your altar, because the altar is your "cross." It is what lifts you up for the world to see. It is what you will die on.

Elijah began repairing the altar by putting *12 stones* in place. Twelve represents foundation and divine election. It is God's number of purpose. Israel is comprised of 12 tribes. The church began with 12 apostles. There were 12 spies sent to look at the Promised Land. Solomon's various building projects involved numbers and measurements of 12. In Heaven, the Tree of Life, which originally stood in the center of the Garden of Eden, will stand in the middle of the eschatological city and bear 12 kinds of fruit every month for the healing of the nations.

Elijah *put the wood in order.* Your altar, if it is to be repaired, must be built according to your divine purpose. You are not here by accident, no matter what your birth certificate says. We had purpose before we became people. Our function preceded our form. We are the called according to the purpose of God. When we see our purpose as wife, mother, minister, servant, scribe, prophet, musician, poet, praise leader, pastor or whatever, we will begin to see which things in our lives are out of order, or "broken down."

Notice that Elijah *made a trench about the altar.* We are a holy, set-aside and consecrated creation. There should be a separation between us and the things of the world. One of the problems in the Church today is that it looks too much like the world. You can't always tell the "saints" from the "ain'ts." Take inventory of your life. Does the world know you're in it and not of it? Are your finances as mismanaged as the slothful of the world? Are your children listening to women being maligned and denigrated in rap music just like the world's children? Are you allowing the same pornographic cable programming into your home as the world allows? Are your skirts as high-cut and blouses as low-cut as the queens of the world? Single sister, do you have condoms under your mattress "just in case" like the ladies in the world? The Word says Elijah made the trench around the altar "as great as would contain two measures of seed." The distinction between you and the world should be noticeable if nothing else.

Then the prophet laid the sacrifice up on the altar and saturated it with *water.* Scripture says he *poured it on the burnt sacrifice and on the wood.* He even filled the trench with water. Water represents the cleansing and purifying power of the Word of God. Make sure that every area of your life is soaked with the truth of God's Word. Don't allow anything to remain untouched by it. Even the "trench" between you and the world should be filled with the Word. That way if anybody wants to get close to you, they're going to have to get "wet" to do it!

> *And it came to pass at the time of the offering...that Elijah the prophet came near, and said, Lord...let it be known this day that Thou art God in Israel, and that I am Thy servant, and that I have done all these things at Thy word. Hear me, O Lord,*

hear me, that this people may know that Thou art the Lord
God, and that Thou hast turned their heart back again
(1 Kings 18:36-37).

When we present ourselves as living sacrifices, we are not only
the sacrifice, but also the ones making the presentation to God. If
we are to "become" worship, we have to embody the whole
process. Look at the attitude that accompanied Elijah's actions. He
was *humble*. He declared before the entire assembly that everything
he had done was according to the Word of God and for the purpose of turning the people's hearts back to God. God didn't put
you here for your good pleasure; He put you here for His. He did-
n't bless you for your benefit; He blessed you so you could become
a blessing to others. Complete worship, total worship, *true* worship, is that which fulfills the great commandment to love the Lord
with all your heart, mind, soul and might, and to love your neigh-
bor as yourself. Jesus said every law is fulfilled in those two. (See
Mark 12:28-31.)

Elijah was also *expectant*. Once he knew he had done everything he was instructed to do, just like Abraham and others before
him, he waited for God to do His part. You don't have to wonder
if God is going to do miraculous things in your life. When true
worship takes place, it is God's pleasure to show up and show out!
Have you ever seen God smile? You will when you devote yourself
to making your life an offering unto Him.

Then the fire of the Lord fell, and consumed the burnt sacrifice,
and the wood, and the stones, and the dust, and licked up the
water that was in the trench. And when all the people saw it,
they fell on their faces: and they said, The Lord, He is the God;
the Lord, He is the God (1 Kings 18:38-39).

This is what happens when God smiles. The miracle at Mount
Carmel is a thrilling testimony of God's faithfulness to honor a life
that lives the Word of God, does the works of God and becomes
worship unto God. *The fire fell.* You know God has shown up when
the unusual takes place. Only God could make fire fall *down*. Light
a match and turn it upside down. The flame will still point up. But
when God is in the fire, it falls down, just like it fell at Pentecost,
just like it will fall on you when your life is lined up according to
His Word, His will and His way.

Scripture says that when the fire fell on Elijah's sacrifice, it *"consumed the burnt sacrifice, and the wood, and the stones, and the dust, and licked up the water that was in the trench."* God wants to be pleased with your whole life, not just part of it. He doesn't want you to hold anything back from Him because He will use it all to glorify Himself in the world.

Sometimes people who walk with God and do His will find themselves in hopeless, painful, discouraging circumstances. That is part of the journey. Sometimes it may not seem like God can do anything with your marriage, your health, your career, your children or your life. You may have thought you had everything in order, but now everything seems lifeless. Don't despair. That's just water. Remember, woman of God, we can't make wet wood burn. In the world, we use water to put out fires. But God uses water to start fires! Yes, things look a little bleak, but that will be only for a season, while He's getting everything in your life nice and saturated. Then watch out, because the fire's about to fall! Just like that day at Mount Carmel, when *all the people saw it* and *fell on their faces*, your life will be such a glorious witness to the power of God that others will come running to your flaming altar crying, "What must I do to be saved?"

When God consumed Elijah's sacrifice at Mount Carmel, nothing was left but ashes. There is nothing in your life that wasn't planned by, directed by and controlled by God. He'll use every good, bad, blessed and cursed thing in your life to His glory. He's even going to use the ashes. The ashes are the best part, as you'll see in the next chapter.

From My Heart

For as the rain cometh down, and the snow from heaven, and returneth not thither, but watereth the earth, and maketh it bring forth and bud, that it may give seed to the sower, and bread to the eater: so shall My word be that goeth forth out of My mouth: it shall not return unto Me void, but it shall accomplish that which I please, and it shall prosper in the thing whereto I sent it (Isaiah 55:10-11).

This is the promise of worship. We become the very word that goes forth from the mouth of God. If you're not sure what true worship looks like, make a conscious, quality decision to become a living epistle that is "walking Word."

Choose a Scripture you want to become true in your life. Write it below. Then sincerely pray and ask God to make it "you." It is His heart's desire to make His Word true in you, so pray with expectation, not doubting.

The Word: _____

_____

_____

- *HEAR IT*   • *HIDE IT*   • *HARVEST IT*

Remember that faith without *works* is dead, and dead faith can't please God. Look for opportunities to put God's Word into action. Submit to it first in your own life. Then others can see it, and you will be able to pass the blessing of it on to them.

- *OBEY IT*   • *DISPLAY IT*   • *RELAY IT*

Look for God to show up when you become *worship*. He will confirm and affirm His Word in you, and He'll do it in a way that will change you forever.

- *BELIEVE IT*   • *BEHAVE IT*   • *BEHOLD IT*

From Your Heart

Meditate on the following passages:

Hear ye the word of the Lord...little children...O Lord...Order my steps in Thy word...Thy word is very pure...Uphold me according unto Thy word...O daughter of Zion...thou art Mine...being fruitful in every good work...Thou art my King, O God...I will delight myself in Thy statutes...My meat is to do the will of Him that sent Me, and to finish His work...worship the Lord in the beauty of holiness...love the Lord...Ye are the temple of the living God...Behold...the fire which is upon the altar...behold, the glory of the Lord...God dwelleth in us...Hallelujah!

Take some time to consider the different names of God, Jesus and the Holy Spirit (Jehovah-jireh, Almighty God, King, Lamb of God, Emmanuel, The Comforter, The Spirit of Truth, Anointing, Living Water, etc.). Write down three names *for each Person* that speak to you the most. Then tell the Lord in worshipful prayer why He is worthy to be called each name. Don't shortchange Him. Worship as long as your heart has something to say about a particular name. Don't allow anything or anybody to interrupt you. Turn off the phone or leave the house if you have to. God is always worth your full, undivided attention...because you will certainly have His.

Chapter Six

Exodus...Exchange...Excess

Even as God uses you, anoints you and directs you to bring healing to other broken, fragmented, tormented persons, you can and will be hurt yourself. When that day arrives, God doesn't want you—His good but hurting soldier—to despair. He wants you to know that He specializes in turning setbacks into triumphs, stumbling blocks into stepping stones and every curse into a blessing. His word to you when you are wounded, weary, worried and tired of waiting, is, "Don't panic. Don't run. Don't hide. Don't doubt. Don't fear."

When Jesus was wounded for our transgressions and beaten for our healing, He was weak, He was broken, He was hurting, He was feverish, achy, sore and in pain. All diseases and sins were dumped onto Him at one time—all viruses, all disorders, all problems, all needs, *all, all, all*! On Calvary, He was physically at His worst...and God chose that moment to use His Son to save the world.

We become our greatest in God when we hurt from the many wounds we experience in the war against the enemy of our souls. We're able to stand tall, firm and faithful to see to the healing of others when we ourselves are suffering the most. God's power is perfected in our weakness. Weakness is not just those things that we suffer at the hands of others; it also includes the diseased condition of our hearts, the ugliness of unforgiveness in us, the bad habits we are determined to hold onto and the dark behaviors we can't explain or control. Weakness is, simply defined, our frailty as fallen creatures.

Ironically, it is our weaknesses that make us want to walk in our own power. When we see ourselves as vulnerable (weak), we get scared and try to take control of our circumstances to keep from getting hurt. But God wants us to turn to Him and use His power when we're weak. He wants us to remember our position as His daughter, wife and vessel. He seeks to remind us daily that He is a very present help and that He alone can save us from every flood that attempts to overtake us. O daughter, how often would He gather us together even as a hen gathers her chicks under her wings, and we would not! We don't always take the Lord up on His offer to take care of us. Why? Because in order to get His power, we have to give up our own. In order for His Kingdom to come, ours has to go, and we're not always willing to do that. But if we are called to be women behind power—and we are—then every bit of our power must be surrendered to Him.

The process of allowing God to overcome our weakness with His power is—like all of God's gifts of grace—progressive in nature. He exposes only enough weakness for us to be able to hand over to Him. Then when we do, He shows us the power He has given to us to be free from it. When we use that power by faith, we are rewarded with the blessing of His divine nature in the place of our weakness. Having brought us to a new level of strength in Him, He's then able to expose the deeper issues of our heart to us.

God uses power to release us from the bondage of sin, which is our weakness, and birth us into holy, peaceful, joyful, powerful living. This happens in an ongoing cycle of *exodus*, *exchange*, and *excess*. Exodus is God's way of delivering us from the captivity of our weakness. Exchange is God's way of divesting us of the baggage associated with our captivity. Excess is that state of abundance enjoyed by God's children when God dwells in us at a new level of power.

Exodus

Many are the afflictions of the righteous: but the Lord delivereth him out of them all (Psalm 34:19).

Did you know that our weaknesses were not designed to destroy us, but rather to strengthen us? Those frailties, fractures and faults that plague us, hinder and hurt us were assigned by satan to take us out. But that which satan means for evil, will always turn out for our good. Many will be saved by our scarred lives if we will just hold onto the hand of the One sent daily to deliver us.

No saint is exempt from pain. Everyone has been beaten, cut, stabbed, betrayed or abused at one time or another. Some of you are dripping blood from wounds as you read this, while others sit with phony smiles—the plastic look of success—because your wounds are deep mental and emotional ones from the past. All of us are either walking with a spiritual limp, wearing a spiritual cast or brace, have wrapped ourselves in spiritual bandages or are in the midst of spiritual open-heart surgery. We are bruised or hemorrhaging, internally or externally, because our self-esteem or our self-image—"who God says we are"—has been stomped on, buried, denounced or denied by the enemy through our mothers, our fathers, our siblings, spouses, in-laws (acting like outlaws), church folks, job folks, television and music video folks and ex-relationship folks.

Learn one important fact about your Christian walk before you continue (and you must continue). At any given moment, you will be able to declare one of three things regarding pain:

"I have been hurt."
"I am hurting right now."
"I will be hurting."

In fact, the Bible declares that they who live godly shall suffer persecution (see 2 Tim. 3:12), meaning we will suffer pain, be injured and get mistreated and talked about. Sometimes it can be overwhelming. But as sure as your name is what it is, God is a deliverer. He is the Deliverer. He sees you in your bondage. He knows that you are powerless to help yourself. And He has already mapped out your exodus.

Now, you may wonder if exodus is even necessary. After all, a lot of people function all right without deliverance. You've been doing all right without your deliverance. God has been able to serve, heal and love others through you. Dealing with your issues might hurt more than it helps. It will hurt, no doubt. But you should know that God is not just trying to help you; He wants to heal you. Helping you would maintain you in your current circumstances. But God wants to take you to a new level in Him and with Him. He's not offering you an attitude adjustment; He's offering an *altitude adjustment*. He wants to take you higher, woman of God, and in order to do that, He must release you from every tether that grounds you. Anything that hinders you from soaring as high as you can needs to be cut away from you.

Exodus is necessary if we truly want to walk in God's power. Where the Spirit of the Lord is, there is liberty, or freedom (see 2 Cor. 3:17). When we possess the Spirit of the Lord, we possess His power. No freedom, no power. And when we have no power, the devil can come in and take control. That's right; no freedom means no power, and no power means we have no freedom.

Exodus begins with three declarations:

"I should get out"
"I can get out."
"I will get out."

First, we must recognize our need for exodus. No one tries to escape anything that doesn't seem like a prison. That's why satan will try to dress up your mess and make it look like Shangri-La; he wants to keep you from trying to get out of it. We can be laughing, singing, lifting up our hands during praise and worship and be as sapped of life inside as Ezekiel's valley of dry bones.

> *The hand of the Lord was upon me, and carried me out in the spirit of the Lord, and set me down in the midst of the valley which was full of bones, and caused me to pass by them round about: and, behold, there were very many in the open valley; and, lo, they were very dry. And He said unto me, Son of man, can these bones live? And I answered, O God, Thou knowest* (Ezekiel 37:1-3).

When you are hurt, wounded, crushed or broken, a good place to be is in a valley with God. If you can get to God in your valley, everything is subject to change at any moment. In one moment, you can go from poverty to prosperity. In one moment, you can go from homeless to homeowner. In one moment, you can leap from sickness to health, depression to delight. In one moment, you can make your exodus into freedom. Why? Because if you are willing to see them, God will show you your dry bones!

Dry bones are injured, wounded, disconnected foundations and structures in our lives. Our physical bones give our bodies shape and stability. Marriage, family relationships, self-perception, a sense of purpose, ministry—these are all things that help make up the "shape" of us. God asked Ezekiel if the bones could live—be healed, revived or restored—and the prophet's response was, "Thou knowest." Once we recognize that there are damaged and dead areas in our lives, the next step is to admit that we can't fix them and trust God to tell us what is in His heart about how they should be brought back to life. We know we should get out of our current position or disposition, and we understand that God is the only way.

Once we realize that exodus is necessary, we must know that it is possible. We can get to that new level of healing, or success, or knowledge. We can, through Christ, do all things, including embrace our exodus. We can take our purpose, our destiny and our anointing, and we can become the woman of God we were born to be. That is accomplished by knowing who we are, warts and all. Until we are honest with ourselves and others about the things we should be praised and pitied for, we won't be able to take that path to exodus, because we won't be able to see it. God shows us the truth. Until we are willing to see the truth, we can't see the blessings the truth has to offer us.

Secondly, we should know what God says about us. We are more than conquerors, and we possess One in us who is greater than "he that is in the world" (1 Jn. 4:4). We are fearfully and wonderfully made, and we have destiny. Our steps were ordered by God before the world was set on its axis. We don't have to manufacture a ministry, a marriage, a career or relationships. If we live on the path God has laid out for us, we'll run into everything God has for us in due season.

Part of understanding your ability to experience exodus is knowing when to take the lead and when to allow God to stretch you as you follow. Again, only God can tell you which season you're in. *O Lord God, Thou knowest.* Pursue peace always, and His voice will always be discernable from the devil's and even your own. You'll always know if you should be letting patience have her perfect work or enlarging your tent. You also should always be ready for change and ready to change. Changes may stretch you, but they are necessary in exodus. You may have to put some things down, let some things go or go in a different direction. Do what you have to. Exodus is your step to reaching the prosperity God desires for you. You can't steal second base with your foot on first base. Risk failure in your race to succeed rather than guarantee failure by refusing to run.

Your ability to "come out" of whatever has you in bondage will depend to a large degree on your ability to "come clean." Confession, repentance and consistent washing of your mind and heart by the water of the Word will keep the path of exodus ever visible to your searching eyes. God is a holy God, and He would sooner withhold every blessing He has for you than allow you to defile His holiness. So your exodus may be put on hold if you're holding onto some sinful habit or behavior. God's arm is not shortened, but if you had hoped that you were going to steal a blessing from God without mounting the steep path of personal repentance in wholehearted surrender to God, you are absolutely mistaken. The cross, the blood, and the Word can untangle every mess, straighten every crooked path and work out every difficulty in your life. But you've got to be willing to come clean. Release your sin through confession, reform your conduct and reprogram your character to ensure that you stay on the road to deliverance.

Finally, exodus is a matter of faith. You have to believe that God intends to deliver you, no matter what things look like. Despite appearances, you must remember that God never lets anything happen unless it's loaded with an opportunity to bring Him glory or honor. Mary and Martha found that out when their brother Lazarus took ill. Jesus said, "This sickness is not unto death, but for the glory of God, that the Son of God might be glorified thereby" (Jn. 11:4). God will allow you to go through death and hell to get His much-deserved glory. If what you need in life gives glory to God and you can believe, you will receive. If you can show God faith, He'll follow you anywhere—to the sick room, to the courtroom, to the cemetery, to a prison...anywhere.

Exodus will be used by God to test your faith. God already knows how much faith you have; He just wants *you* to know. So He'll usually test you with a request to see if you're willing to part with your preconceived ideas about your issues, your pain, your broken heart or your confusion. Jesus told Martha, "Take ye away the stone." Martha told Jesus, "Lord, by this time he stinketh: for he hath been dead four days" (Jn. 11:39). "No, Lord." How many times have we said what is surely the most utilized oxymoron in the Kingdom of God? Those two words can't coexist. If you can say "no" to Him, then He's not your "Lord," is He? "No, Lord, he stinks!" No, Lord, my marriage can't be saved. *It stinks!* No, Lord, my relationship with my teenage children can't be restored. *It stinks!* No, Lord, my reputation can't be revived. *It stinks!*

Often, in order to guarantee our exodus, Jesus has to preach to our unbelief. "Said I not unto thee," He tells Martha, "that, if thou wouldest believe, thou shouldest see the glory of God?" (Jn. 11:40) When the Word comes, obey, or you'll never see your deliverance. When Martha obeyed, then, and only then did Jesus call Lazarus—the dead man—to life. Your faith, fleshed out with obedience, is your ticket on the "Exodus Express."

Sometimes we are picked out (even though it seems like we're being picked *on*) to bring glory to God. As believers and students of the Word, we must get to the place where we realize that our trials, troubles and temptations are like turbulent winds. Responded to wrongly, they can destroy us. Responded to spiritually, they can strengthen our lives, causing us to fly higher, to see more, elevating us above storms and helping us fly faster and for longer stretches between rest breaks. The power of a woman of God to rise above pressures—the power of her deliverance—is found in her identification with the death, burial and resurrection of Christ.

Paul put it like this: "That I may know [Jesus], and the power of His resurrection, and the fellowship of His sufferings, being made conformable unto His death; if by any means I might attain unto the resurrection of the dead" (Phil. 3:10-11). How did Jesus die? He died knowing He'd get up again. So every time satan sends an assignment that kills some of your hope, your dreams, your relationships or your ministry, die knowing you will get up again. David had the right idea in Psalm 124:6-7 when he declared:

> *Blessed be the Lord, who hath not given us as a prey to their teeth. Our soul is escaped as a bird out of the snare of the fowlers: the snare is broken, and we are escaped.*

The snare, or trap, of your pain is broken. David says that it's broken and we are free. Exodus is ours when we trust the power of God to deliver us. Certainly we will have scars; they are a part of the journey. In our bondage, scars represent hurt and hindrance. But in exodus, scars represent healing and give us a reason to shout "Hallelujah!"

Exchange

> *Thou hast turned for me my mourning into dancing: Thou hast put off my sackcloth, and girded me with gladness; to the end that my glory may sing praise to Thee, and not be silent. O Lord my God, I will give thanks unto Thee for ever* (Psalm 30:11-12).

All right, you've got your freedom. What do you do with it? What can you do with it? In fact, now that you think about it, you're not even sure you've actually "come out." You're a born-again believer. You've repented and been washed in the blood of the Lord Jesus and with the water of baptism. You're filled with the Holy Ghost...but you're lost in sin. You've been set free, but you're still miserable at times, still impoverished at times, still struggling with addictions. You're singing on the praise team, making a joyful noise, but when you go home, your praise turns to depression. Free enough to shout "Amen!" at the preacher, but angry. Free to fellowship, but full of bitterness.

You're like the little puppy who was chained to a front porch when his owners moved away. The chain, attached to his collar, was just four feet long. His movement was restricted to an area of only four feet in any direction. Every time he tried to run and play, the chain would jerk him back. Every time he tried to jump beyond the four feet, he would choke and gasp for air. Eventually he gave up trying to jump or run.

Then new owners took over the property and set him free, but because he was conditioned to just four feet of space for so long, that's as far as he would go even unchained...until the one who freed him "told" him he was free by taking him by the paws and pulling him past his four-foot boundary. Only then did the dog understand what being free was all about.

The transition from exodus to power always takes us through a transitional season of exchange. Exchange is the place where we trade our old attitudes for new ones. It is the place where we learn that we truly are healed and headed for happiness. When we go through seasons of exchange, we allow our minds and hearts to catch up to our circumstances. God has delivered us from that abusive marriage, from that job, from that addiction, from that unholy affection. We are no longer slaves to our sins, appetites and neediness. Still, we have to shake off the "slave mentality" that will find us, by force of habit, returning to our old ways of doing things. Then we become easy prey for satan, who will tell us that we really aren't delivered; we didn't get freed, cured or fixed, so we may as well go back to doing what we've always done. We're more likely to believe him until God takes us through the process of exchange.

Exchange always takes place in the wilderness, away from old influences, away from the temptation to turn back. God takes us to the wilderness to solidify our deliverance. Of course, in our wilderness, we don't always look "delivered." In fact, we look alone, forsaken and unloved by God. But the wilderness of exchange is necessary if we're going to operate in God's power, for it is the place where we learn to depend on God and God alone. There are rocks in the wilderness that we exchange for a glass of water when we're thirsty. The hard ground delivers up manna when we're hungry, or quail if we get a little particular with our hunger. In the wilderness, we're lost, but led by God. We're poor, but provided for by God. We're afraid, but protected by God. We're lonely, but we are comforted by God...if we want to be. Exchange is never forced on us. Manna was available, but Israel was never required to eat it. If God is trying to teach you how to depend on Him, though, it's not likely you'll find much else to eat in your wilderness.

The wilderness is unavoidable; every exodus leads to a season of exchange. Deliverance, to be complete, must go beyond what we can see in the natural. You may not be doing what you used to do, but God wants to deliver you from the desire to do it. He wants to eliminate any chance that you'll turn back. Exodus 13:17-18 says God took the children of Israel into their wilderness for that very reason. Look at the passage in the New Living Translation:

> *When Pharaoh finally let the people go, God did not lead them on the road that runs through Philistine territory, even though that was the shortest way from Egypt to the Promised Land. God said, "If the people are faced with a battle, they might change their minds and return to Egypt." So God led them along a route through the wilderness toward the Red Sea...*

Usually the difficulty you face after making the decision to accept your deliverance from God is nothing more than a divine detour designed to keep you headed in the right direction, even when it seems like the wrong one. You let God deliver you from that toxic work environment. Now you find out on top of all your new financial problems that you've got to have surgery. You think God is mad at you, but He knew that a couple more weeks of bologna sandwiches would have driven you to beg for your old job back. Now you can't go back to that job or any job. You are totally dependent on Him—and Jehovah-jireh will provide. You'll see.

The need for exchange may not obvious to us at first. That's because the reason for exodus—that is, the thing that put us in our "Egypt"—isn't always obvious. Israel ended up in Egypt because Joseph was there. After his hardships with Potiphar and prison, Pharaoh had exalted him and put him in charge of all Egypt. Once he was reunited with his brothers, he decided to move his whole family there. Pharaoh gave them the best land in Egypt and gave his brothers positions of authority. Israel prospered in Egypt long after Joseph and his family was gone. In fact, they prospered so much that the new Egyptian king—who didn't know anything about Joseph—became afraid of them and made them slaves. He was so cruel to them that their cries reached the ears of God, who sent Moses to deliver them. But Israel wouldn't have been in Egypt in the first place except for the sin of Joseph's brothers. Their jealousy of him made them sell him into slavery...*in Egypt*! It was not Egypt's sin that put Israel in bondage, but Israel's.

Why is this important? Because the people who were oppressed in Egypt didn't move there and become slaves. They were born there. They were there because of the actions of their fathers' fathers. Some of you are suffering from the sins of your mama's mama and your daddy's daddy. Grandpa hit grandma, so your father hits your mother, and they both hit you. Now, because you don't know any better, you don't think that man you're living with loves you unless he's hitting on you. Mama married a weak man and emasculates him, because daddy was weak, because granddaddy walked out on grandma, and the only way she knew how to raise 12 boys was to keep her foot on their necks.

So you've got issues, girl. No matter how determined you were to do things differently than your angry, bitter mother did, you find yourself turning into her. You married this man you love so dearly, and a monster you never saw rose up in you. Now he's wondering what happened to the sweet gentle spirit he said, "I do," to...and you can't tell him, because you don't know where she is either. So you trusted God for your exodus, and now you find yourself in the wilderness, afraid and fighting the urge to go back to Egypt...but you're struggling. That's a sure sign that you need to make your way to God's exchange counter and do some trading.

When Israel left Egypt, the Bible says the Egyptians were so anxious to see them go that they loaded them up with "jewels of silver, and jewels of gold, and raiment." It says, "the Lord gave the people favour in the sight of the Egyptians, so that they lent unto them such things as they required. And they spoiled the Egyptians." (See Exodus 12:35-36.) That word *spoil* means they looted the Egyptians. We see that passage and rejoice. Praise the Lord, the wealth of the wicked folks in Egypt was stored up for the righteous little children of Israel! But consider another point of view. Let's say your "Egypt" is a homosexual lifestyle. You asked God to deliver you from it, and He did. But every once in awhile, you have an evil, nagging desire to cruise by a gay bar. That "Jones" you still have for that which used to give you such pleasure is your "loot" from Egypt.

You're a grown woman now, but every time you hear a man raise his voice, you're a little girl again, hiding in the closet, afraid that your drunk, violent daddy is going to find you and beat you before he passes out. Loot. You told yourself you would never allow yourself to be used by men the way your mother was. You forgot to remind yourself about that promise when "he" knocked on your door at 11 p.m., because he had to wait for his wife to go to bed before he could creep over to your house. Loot. You're not doing drugs anymore, but you're drinking. Loot. You're not drinking, but you're eating yourself to death. Loot. You're not overeating, but you're bulimic. Loot. You don't have eating issues, but all your credit cards are "maxed" out because you can't stop shopping. You're running out of loot because of your *loot*!

Why would God let us leave Egypt with baggage that He knew would harm us? God is nothing if not thorough. He'll let you take your spoils out of Egypt as long as you get out of Egypt. Then He will use the wilderness to destroy the spoils and your craving for it. That way you won't ever have to go back to Egypt looking for it. Then if God ever has to send you back to Egypt to deliver somebody who is in the same bondage you were in, you won't be tempted to stay there. He delivered you from those sexual addictions, but He let you take your pornographic magazines out of Egypt. Now that you've spent some time in your wilderness, learning about the faithfulness of God, you've lost the desire for anything that doesn't please Him. The magazines can go in the trash. You've got that testimony to share with another sister suffering in her Egypt. There is deliverance, and there is healing too.

God wants you delivered completely so He can guide you into your Promised Land. He prepared it for you before He made you. He made you so that you would enter it. It is your destiny, and it is more than eye can see, ear can hear or heart can imagine.

For the Lord thy God bringeth thee into a good land, a land of brooks of water, of fountains and depths that spring out of valleys and hills; a land of wheat, and barley, and vines, and fig trees, and pomegranates; a land of oil olive, and honey; a land wherein thou shalt eat bread without scarceness, thou shalt not lack any thing in it; a land whose stones are iron, and out of whose hills thou mayest dig brass (Deuteronomy 8: 7-9).

Your Promised Land is anything God has earmarked for you. It is yours because He has prepared it for you, and He takes you through your wilderness to prepare you for it. If you want to be blessed, do a Bible study on Israel's acquisition of the Promised Land from Egypt until their possession. You should know how the Lord led them, loved them, provided for them, changed them, chastised them and cherished them. You should know that He swore they would have the land, even before they were in bondage. You should know that for every moment of their 40 years of wandering, God never once abandoned them no matter how many times they accused Him of it. You should know how He guided them and protected them, then led them in every battle required to possess their land. He tried their faith in the wilderness. He developed their character in the wilderness. He brought them low in the wilderness so He could exalt them as a nation and as a people. You should know all this because He wants to do the same things for you if you'll let Him. When you let Him make every exchange He needs to make in you, your possession is certain. If you don't, you are unprepared to perceive, possess or protect your promise.

Anything you need to exchange with God in the wilderness falls into one of three categories. You've got pride that you need to exchange for a new humility. You've got shame that you need to exchange for a new identity. You've got fear that you need to exchange for a new fortress. Every issue you face, at its core, will be one of those three things. And if you want to walk in the power of God, you have to make the exchange. If you don't, you've told God that you're willing to let Him handle some things, but not all things. Then the more the issue plagues you, the more you'll struggle and complain and beg to go back to Egypt. An entire generation of Israel missed the Promised Land like that. Don't miss your blessing.

When you suffer with an issue of pride, you have said, in essence, "I *deserve* the promises of God." In saying that, you reject the grace of God. Grace is comprised of those things that God gives even though we don't deserve them. Salvation is a gift of God's grace. We don't deserve it, and yet He offers it to us. Grace is God's drawing nigh to us and lovingly bestowing His blessings on us. Often our deliverance from our sin will make us puffed up, especially if we're a little unsure of our liberty and there are others around who are worse off than we are to make us feel better about ourselves. But God says He resists the proud (see Jas. 4:6). He sets Himself up on whatever side the prideful person is not on, so He can knock them down a peg or two. God can't bless us with His grace when we're prideful. That's why He stands ready with a healthy dose of humility for us in our wilderness. God gives grace to the humble, so He gives humility to the proud, because He loves them too.

When we're struggling with shame, we are telling the world, "I *don't deserve* the promises of God." In saying that, we are rejecting God's mercy, which is new to us daily if we'll receive it. Grace is God's giving to us what we don't deserve. Mercy, on the other hand, is the act of God's *not* giving to us what we *do* deserve. The wages of sin is death. But God is merciful to us sinners who offend His holiness daily. When we reject God's mercy, it is because we don't understand or accept our new identity in Him. We are new creatures in Christ, heirs to the divine nature of God. He has blessed us with the privilege of housing His Spirit in us. If we don't accept that, we will never accept His power or use it. Shame is the devil's attempt to make us impotent in the Kingdom of God. If he can get us to hang our heads, we'll never seek the Father above because we'll think we don't have the right to. Shame will make us hide ourselves from others, putting the truth of who we are in the dark, where satan has complete control over it. However, when we decide to walk in our new identity as set-aside, sanctified saints, our shame becomes a shout, because we look back and see just how far God has brought us from our Egypt.

Fear says, "I *don't believe* the promises of God." That is a rejection of God Himself because we're calling the One who is the Truth a liar. When we reject God, we reject all that God has to offer us, except His mercy and His grace. Those endure forever. But when we reject God, we can't call on Him in prayer. We can't enjoy personal communion with Him. We lose the gifts of His Spirit, gifts like long-suffering, peace, discernment, self-control, wisdom and patience. We lose our power in Him when we reject Him.

Sadly, fear is at the root of all our issues of pride and shame, which are actually two sides to the same pitiful coin. Both are ungodly preoccupations with "self," one giving us an over-inflated view of ourselves, the other under-inflating our view. Both are lies, which makes them both contrary to God's will for us.

The only way to free ourselves from fear is to determine to make God our fortress. When we dwell in Him by faith and allow Him to dwell in us, we learn in our wilderness that He will never leave us or forsake us. When God is our fortress, fear ceases to find a home in us. When God is our fortress, we give His perfect love permission to evict our fear.

The wildernesses in our lives are deliberately and strategically placed there so God can exchange every weight and sin, which hinders us or saps our strength, for His presence and His promises. Exchange is God's way of guaranteeing that we will keep every blessing He gives. Isaiah 35 shows us a wonderful portrait of the exchange that takes place in the wilderness with God. Isaiah 35:1-2 says, "The wilderness and the solitary place shall be glad...and the desert shall rejoice, and blossom as the rose. It shall blossom abundantly, and rejoice even with joy and singing...." In other words, on your way to your Promised Land, your wilderness can be a place of beauty and richness.

Excess

How do you know when you've entered your Promised Land? How do you know you're truly walking in the power that goes along with it? You'll know when nothing you do is done by your own power. You'll know because everything you touch will become bigger than you were trying to make it. Excess is the gift of God to those who wholeheartedly embrace their exodus and endure the exchanges that need to take place in the wilderness. When we live in excess, we are living "exceeding abundantly above all that we ask or think, according to the power that worketh in us" (Eph. 3:20), and that power is itself "exceeding great."

Living in excess is not the same as living *to* excess. The latter is living beyond what is decently acceptable just for pride's sake. The former is living according to God's riches, according to God's plan and for God's glory alone. Excess is different from success as well in that success is achievable through our own efforts. Living in excess requires total surrender to God and a total willingness to work through every issue that might prevent us from reaching the mark set for us by Him. The focus of success is on possessions, yachts, gorgeous homes, big cars, fancy clothes and large bank accounts. In excess, it is possible to have all these things, but they are not the goal. Success buys a house, while excess buys a home. Success can buy you a bed, but excess seeks to give you rest. Success buys what it wants. Excess wants what it buys.

When we live according to the excess of God, we are not concerned with using our power to gain position, prestige and popularity. We may enjoy these things, but they won't define us. A person living in excess is defined by and directed by God in all her efforts. Goals are dictated by the desires placed in the heart of that person by God, and she can move toward them with confidence, knowing that God will prosper everything she puts her hand to. It is said that Alexander the Great went out with his armies to conquer the nations of the world. After the last victorious battle ended, history tells us that Alexander wept because there were no more worlds left to conquer. He had achieved all his self-set goals, but he did not find abiding satisfaction. A woman living in excess goes after the things of God, and since God is infinite, so too are the possibilities within her reach.

The only hindrance to our living in excess would be our lack of desire to do so. God's desire for us is that we would live not according to our own strength, but according to His. He wants us to seek peace that passes our understanding and joy that we're unable to articulate in our finitude. God wants us to exceed the expectations of men. If we weren't supposed to live beyond our ability, our wisdom or the limits of our desires and imagination, Jesus could have stayed in Heaven. Instead, He came down to earth, lived, died, rose and sent us His power by which to live. Excess is ours if we'll go after it—and it is God's desire that we go after it, for a number of reasons.

First of all, everything God creates has purpose and value to Him. That includes you. He made you in His image, after His form and likeness. You are the object of God's attention and affection and He wants the best for you, but not the best you can provide;

He wants to give you the best *He* can provide. Your life will change completely when you understand how much God cares for you. He has placed at your disposal an unlimited wealth of resources. As the owner of everything in the universe, God wants to make sure His children lack nothing. He intends for us to make full use of everything He has given to us. As His supreme creation, God makes His own wisdom available to you as well as His power and His sensitivity. Peter says we have been given everything we need for life and godliness (see 2 Pet. 1:3).

Your prosperity has always been on God's mind. Very early on in the Word of God, it is established as a worthwhile goal. The Lord's first promise to Abraham was a promise of abundance.

Now the Lord had said unto Abram, Get thee out of thy country, and from thy kindred, and from thy father's house, unto a land that I will show thee: and I will make of thee a great nation, and I will bless thee, and make thy name great; and thou shalt be a blessing: and I will bless them that bless thee, and curse him that curseth thee: and in thee shall all families of the earth be blessed (Genesis 12:1-3).

One man would become a great nation with a great name. A man without a home would become a blessing to others. In this one man, who had been told to leave his family, all the families of the earth would be blessed. Abraham was so special to God that God threatened to curse anyone who cursed him and promised to bless anyone who blessed him. This is what happens when we live under the umbrella of the Lord's excess. Abraham was doing fine right where he was, but God didn't want him to do "fine"; He wanted excess. Scripture is full of accounts of men and women who, by the power of God, are led to abundant living for God's glory. Either you believe the Word, or you don't. If you accept the Bible as truth, then you must believe God wants us to be blessed and to prosper.

Excess is not without its purpose. One obvious reason God blesses us the way He does is so that our lives are on display. He wants our lives to serve as examples of what His love and power can do for anyone who trusts Him. By sending His prosperity into the lives of His children, God can demonstrate to an unbelieving world His nature and His power. Paul wrote, "God hath chosen the weak things of the world to confound the things which are mighty" (1 Cor. 1:27b). Abraham served as an example to each of us of what God wants for His children. "And if ye be Christ's, then are ye Abraham's seed, and heirs according to the promise" (Gal. 3:29). In other words, we're in Abraham's family, so what God promised him, God promised us.

Moreover, God wants you blessed so you can provide for your family's needs. The Bible makes it clear that we must provide for the material as well as the spiritual needs of our families. God gets no glory if your family has to live in a rat-breeding, roach-infested tenement. He is not pleased if your family never has enough to eat, or if your children wear hand-me-downs or go without shoes. He is a God of abundance of blessings. He wants you to avail yourself of His generous spirit.

Finally, God wants you to live in excess to support and under-gird His work in the world. As God sends prosperity into your life, He not only meets your need, but He also makes it possible for you to help carry out the Great Commission to "go ye into all the world, and preach the gospel to every creature" (Mk. 16:15). Some-times money in the hands of an unbeliever is a snare, but money in the hands of a believer can be a tool to do God's will.

As Christians prosper, financially and otherwise, and use their resources for God's work, good things start to happen. Churches get built. Mission stations are established. Gospel radio and televi-sion programs are produced and aired. Soul-winning ministries are launched to share the message of salvation with those who don't know the God of Exceeding Abundance. These things do take money, so God prospers His people with abundant finances. They take talent, so God endows His people with abundant, useful gifts. They also take people willing to serve, so God has instructed us to pray to "the Lord of the harvest," that He might send us an abundant supply of servants and laborers (Mt. 9:38).

Living in excess is walking in the power of God, seeing by it, hearing by it and seeking it at all times. As women called to pow-erful living, we must allow God to prepare us for excess. David understood that. He acknowledged God's desire to bless him in Second Samuel 7 and declared his house ready to receive whatever blessing God saw fit to bestow. Perhaps the simplest definition of an "excess-ful" life is *knowing and attaining God's goals for your life the way God wants you to know and attain them*. It is becoming what God wants you to become, doing what God wants you to do and possessing what God wants you to own.

Real excess is not a destination; it is a journey. It is movement. It is the joy created by progress and the character cultivated in process. It is not a city where you will arrive tomorrow. It is the enjoyment of today, the "now." Real excess is keeping every schedule God has for you and fulfilling His assignments for your life. Real excess is the ultimate expression of a powerful, Spirit-filled and Spirit-led existence.

From My Heart

The Desires of My Heart

What are the desires beneath your desires? Why do you want that particular job, that specific car or a house on that exact street? Bitterness is usually the result of some unfulfilled desire that has nothing to do with what we think we're disappointed about. A woman who's bitter toward men may say it's because she never gets asked out. But that might be a desire that's covering a deeper desire to feel wanted, loved and accepted. Think about one of your deepest desires and complete the following statement. Don't write right away. Really think about what's in your heart.

Lord, I desire _____, because it will give/make me _____, which will ultimately make me feel _____.

Now take the last part of the statement concerning how you ultimately want to feel. Is it a desire consistent with God's desires for you? If not, the Holy Spirit has just exposed a lie that has been allowed to exist in your heart. Ask God to shed more light on it with the truth of His Word. If it is consistent with the things God desires for you, ask God to grant you that desire in *whatever way He wants to*. He has already promised that He will (see 1 Jn. 5:14-15). You might be surprised to find that your "surface" desires will either cease to be or that He'll grant them beyond your imagination. If you're not sure that what you want is according to God's will, ask Him for wisdom (see Jas. 1:5).

From Your Heart

Meditate on the following passages:

The Lord is my rock, and my fortress, and my deliverer...Blessed is the man to whom the Lord will not impute sin...When I said, My foot slippeth; Thy mercy, O Lord, held me up...My help cometh from the Lord...my hiding place...I found Him whom my soul loveth...The Lord hath given me...beauty for ashes, the oil of joy for mourning, the garment of praise for the spirit of heaviness...O sing unto the Lord a new song...I will seek Him...to see Thy power and Thy glory...and I will dwell in the house of the Lord for ever.

What was your most recent exodus? How did you know you were delivered? What issues did you bring out with you? What has God given you in exchange for your pride, shame or fear? How have your opinions about God changed since your exodus?

_____

_____

_____

_____

_____

_____

_____

_____

_____

Take a moment to praise and thank God for your deliverance.

Chapter Seven

Revelation...Response...Rest

Let us be glad and rejoice, and give honour to Him: for the marriage of the Lamb is come, and His wife hath made herself ready. And to her was granted that she should be arrayed in fine linen, clean and white... (Revelation 19:7-8).

Who are you?

God said, "Behold, I make all things new" (Rev. 21:5). You are the last solution to the last problem that will ever plague this sinful world. You are the magnificent beauty, chosen, born, then reborn to become the cherished bride of the most eligible bachelor in the universe. You are the one He adores. You are the one His Spirit longs to inhabit. He has already given His life for you. On the day you wed, He will give His life *to* you. His Spirit already lives on you and in you, making you hunger and thirst for Him. You run after Him, yearning to "apprehend that for which you were apprehended" (see Phil. 3:12). You chase Him, believing *He'll catch you.*

How did you fall so in love with Him? Better question: How did you ever live without Him? Answer? You didn't. You existed. Your heart was beating, but it didn't ache for anyone's presence like it does for His. You worked, but you didn't seek His purpose in it. You cried but didn't know how to seek comfort. You loved, but you were too afraid to lean. Then He came into your life and all that changed. How did you go so long without being sought after, noticed, protected and paid attention to? How did you ever stand without His support, endure without His encouragement, serve without His humility, walk without His direction or hope without His promises? How did you ever live without His power? You don't remember? Well, God says you're on the right track, then:

> *Forgetting those things which are behind,* [I reach] *forth unto those things which are before* (Philippians 3:13b).

> *Remember ye not the former things, neither consider the things of old. Behold, I will do a new thing; now it shall spring forth; shall ye not know it? I will even make a way in the wilderness, and rivers in the desert* (Isaiah 43:18-19).

Remember to forget. God is doing a new thing for that woman who is willing to let go of her past and reach for her purpose. After all, He didn't give you His power to use in your past. He's not expecting you to go back into yesterday and fix it. His power is there to help you unlock mysteries, not repair histories. If at some point in time between your "then" and your "now" you met Jesus Christ, then every sin, sorrow, past imperfection, mistake and emotional debt was canceled and stamped VOID. It can't be used against you. When you got your power, it came with a promise that nothing could keep you from walking in your destiny.

You can bet, though, that satan is right outside your door, waiting to silence your praise. He sees your debt, and he's trying to discourage you in it. He heard that your child was getting into trouble, and he wants you to get bitter and angry with your baby's daddy. He knows you're tired, worn out and ready to give up. That little nagging feeling on the back of your neck is him; he's trying to push you over the edge. He has enlisted the aid of your family and friends too. They see how hard it is for you. That smile you have on your face can't be real. Your husband is too mean. That peace you seem to walk in has to be fake. Nobody goes through what you've been through and doesn't break down. Why do you keep working at that job where they treat you like that? Why don't you leave your husband? Why do you keep fighting when it's obvious to them that you're losing, and badly at that? Tell them we fight because we haven't lost. And we won't lose as long as we continue in battle. The truth is *we* can't lose, because *we* aren't fighting. This battle is the Lord's.

What does it mean to be a woman behind the power? It means to be always prepared for combat, even if you aren't the one fighting. Combat for God's chosen is very different from that of the world. Even though our triumphs and casualties are seen here, on satan's turf, he knows and God knows that the fight is not with us or among us. The battleground is not earth. The weapons are not carnal. The adversary is not man, the law, racism, disenfranchisement, sexism, drugs, Hollywood or poverty. The war is not worldly. The best soldiers are not the ones wearing the heaviest armor; they are the ones whose tongues are heavy with praise. The enemy won't fall to the thrust and parry of a foil, but to "the blood of the Lamb and the word of our testimony" (see Rev. 12:11). He won't flinch before our angry faces...but he will start shaking in the face of our *rest*.

Warfare for a woman of power, simply put, is rest. I know that seems like an oxymoron to you, like jumbo shrimp, cruel kindness or tough love. But God's plan for us is that we would be as powerful as possible. Power is found most abundantly in rest. Rest is not inactivity; it is, as the writer of Hebrews points out, a ceasing from our own works as we focus our efforts toward pleasing God. The woman at rest is the woman wielding the most power. She is that wife who can take care of a dozen people at the same time and make each one feel like the "favorite." She is the prophet who calls out one case of cancer in a room of thousands. She's the anonymous "angel" who secretly sees to the financial needs of others.

Rest is not what we think of when we think about operating in exceeding great power. We imagine rent veils, split skies, earthquakes and floods. We look for the most powerful woman of God to kick the door down and make her way furiously to the pulpit, slaying saints and flinging demons left and right, the Word of the Lord burning a hole in her anointed belly. But rest, like power, is never about what you can do. It's about what God can do through you. Resting warriors don't have to fight the winds of a storm. They fly above the storm and let the storm fight itself.

There's no greater example of this truth than in Second Chronicles 20 when "the children of Moab, and the children of Ammon, and with them other beside the Ammonites, came against Jehoshaphat to battle" (verse 1). Although the children of Israel knew that they were spiritually favored by God and special to Him, when word came that their enemies were coming to fight them, they did like some of us. They "feared, and set themselves to seek the Lord." That's the first step to enjoying rest. Seek the Lord. Look for a *revelation* of Him in your situation. Jehoshaphat and his people began fasting and praying—and God revealed Himself.

Revelation is the truth as we receive it from God through His Word and by the power of His Holy Spirit. It is the truth that was and is and always will be, but it must become visible to our spirit at a given time. Revelation is crucial, because it gives us both permission and the impetus to change. Without the revelation of the truth, things would remain as they are—and we would see them as we have always seen them. When truth is injected into a situation that seems hopeless, hope is born. What seemed like the end of a story becomes a beginning. For instance, if I see my daughter overtaken by sinful behavior, I may be tempted to give up on her. Then God reveals to me that He wants all of us saved and that if I pray anything according to His will, I shall have it. My baby's trouble, in light of this revelation, becomes an invitation to hope and pray, because I want her saved and I know that God does too. Revelation is truth, and truth is power.

God told Jehoshaphat and Israel where their enemies were located, and He gave them instructions regarding the upcoming battle. Now, His instructions may not be what you want to hear. You may have prepared yourself with the military strategy of the century, with weapons of the century, with fighting soldiers who are second to none, and then God says, "Don't fight, for these enemies you see, you shall see them no more forever," or God may say, "Ye shall not need to fight in this battle: set yourselves, stand ye still, and see the salvation [the power] of the Lord with you, O Judah and Jerusalem: fear not, nor be dismayed; to morrow go out against them: for the Lord will be with you" (2 Chron. 20:17).

Can you imagine? You're ready to fight. You are itching to fight, and then God says you don't need to fight. He tells you to "set yourselves" and "stand still." What do you mean, stand still? This manager at work has sexually harassed me. What do you mean, stand still? This child is getting on my last good nerve. What do you mean, stand still? I have a good case for a lawsuit. Take your cues from your leader. After God said, "Stand still, don't fight this battle," the Bible says King Jehoshaphat "bowed his head with his face to the ground: and all Judah and the inhabitants of Jerusalem fell before the Lord, worshipping the Lord" (2 Chron. 20:18). When God reveals Himself to us, the right *response* can mean the difference between having power and not having it.

Response is not the simple idea of action. Response in this context is that action that we take as a result of the truth revealed to us by God that amplifies or exemplifies that truth. In other words, if the truth revealed is that God is always a provider of needs, then my response may be to quit all the behind-the-scenes maneuvering and deal-making I've been doing to keep my job. Or it may be to stop cheating on my income taxes. My response may be to stand still and watch the Lord deliver me from a particular debt. It may be to step out and start that new business He laid on my heart many years ago.

Response requires us to focus our attention on hearing God. Jesus tells us in Matthew 10:27 to speak in the light what He tells us in darkness and to preach on the housetops what we hear in the ear. The idea is to allow revelation to become reality by our response. If you find a trustworthy God on your journey, respond by believing Him. If He is jealous, respond in faithfulness. If you find Him gracious, be grateful. If you see His mercy, fear Him. If you find God to be anything contrary to the word He has already given, respond by asking Him to show you the truth. God revealed Himself worthy to Israel, and they responded by worshiping Him.

Often, your victory is just a praise, just a worship away. When you obey God and put down your gun, your tongue, your fist, your money, your anger, your hatred or your bitterness and pick up your tambourines, your organs, your pianos, your hand claps, your praise singers, your choirs...when your weapons are in your sacrifice of praise, you will be able to do what Jehoshaphat and Israel did. Without fighting, you will watch your enemies kill each other without your help. Second Chronicles 20:23-24 declares:

For the children of Ammon and Moab stood up against the inhabitants of mount Seir, utterly to slay and destroy them: and when they had made an end of the inhabitants of Seir, every one helped to destroy another. And when Judah [God's warring praisers] *came toward the watch tower in the wilderness, they looked unto the multitude, and, behold, they were dead bodies fallen to the earth, and none escaped.*

"And when Jehoshaphat and his people came to take away the spoil of them, they found among them in abundance both riches with the dead bodies, and precious jewels, which they stripped off for themselves, more than they could carry away: and they were three days in gathering of the spoil, it was so much" (2 Chron. 20:25). Sometimes we need to rest so we'll have enough strength to receive all the blessings that are going to come our way when God fights our battles for us!

Everything God made glorifies Him in some way. In other words, there is nothing made that will not tell us something about God's nature or His relationship with us. He tells us that we are like trees planted by rivers, fruitful and healthy. He wants us to be diligent like ants and trust that He is as solid as a stone, or that He will sustain us like water. We are sheep to His Shepherd, children to a Father. He was broken like bread and poured out like wine for us. Consider also, then, that when God finished making the heavens and the earth, He rested. He created Sabbath. Why? Is it a picture of Him? Is He a God who is resting? Psalm 121:4 says He doesn't sleep. Hebrews 4 tells us why God created a Sabbath.

For He spake in a certain place of the seventh day on this wise, And God did rest the seventh day from all His works....There remaineth therefore a rest to the people of God. For he that is entered into his rest, he also hath ceased from his own works, as God did from His (Hebrews 4:4,9-10).

God created the Sabbath as an illustration of how His people are to live. We are to cease from our own works the way God did from His. What then are we supposed to do? Ephesians 2:10 tells us that when God made us, He gave us good works to do. It says He ordained that we should walk in them. Notice the verse says *should* and not *would*. We don't always choose to walk on the path

God has already laid out for us. But it is there. If we will allow Him to do it, God can and will order our steps. Walking in the way that God laid out for you before He laid the foundations of the world—that is rest. Rest is the sum and substance of power because rest is the fleshing out of God's will.

The goal of warfare in the world is to defeat your enemy. Striving for such a goal would be redundant for you, sister, because your adversary is already defeated. The battle has already been won in the spirit realm. We are called of God to live into that destiny of victory here on earth. By faith we live, move and have our being in the One who has all power over life and death. When we engage in combat with the enemy, we are following steps ordered to victory. Victory is a closer relationship with God, one in which we are so knitted together in spirit that His desires become ours and all desires are granted.

When we rest, we take Christ's yoke upon us and transfer our load onto His shoulders. Our fights become His fights. He takes our pain, tears and worry and gives us joy, peace and praises unto His name. Remember, though, rest is not inactivity. He wants His children victorious. He set up the universe for us to win our battles. You've never seen a Scripture that says, "If you believe, obey and worship God, you *might* prevail." No, I *am* more than a conqueror through Him. (See Romans 8:37.) There's no question, caveat or exception.

Rest occurs when we choose to hear and obey God. Hebrews 4 says the children of Israel did not enter rest because of their unbelief. That word *unbelief* is a word that also means disobedient. In other words, they knew what to do, but they didn't do it. Therefore they did not enter into God's rest. The writer of Hebrews cautions us against their example (see Heb. 3:12).

We're not born resting any more than we're born with power, holiness or truth. In fact, it is part of our sinful nature to resist rest. But rest is available. It appears next to us each morning with God's mercy. Like everything God gives, however, rest won't be forced on us. We have to receive rest like we receive peace, joy and all the other heavenly gifts. We receive it when we hear the truth and believe it by allowing it to change us from the inside out. If I say I believe God about something and my life doesn't bear out that belief, that's not rest. It's rhetoric. So rest, then, is understood by the following formula:

Revelation + Response = Rest

God's power on earth is most clearly seen not so much in what He does as it is in what He could do but doesn't. The same is true of us when we become sons and daughters of God. What we can do is not nearly as impressive a demonstration of our power as making a conscious decision *not* to do what we could do. Every fruit of the Spirit is a portrait of restraint and self-control.

Rest is power under control. When Moses tried to get a look at God, he had to be warned not to get too close. He had to settle for a sidelong glance at the back of God. Some of us can't even get that close. When we surrender ourselves to the Holy Spirit, there is no limit to what He can do in us and through us. However, there is a limit on what some people are ready to see. Some people aren't ready for you to deliver them. Just pray for me in my unemployment, but not too much. I'm beginning to like this time off. Don't focus those spiritual gifts of discernment and prophesy on me too closely. You may see how envious and jealous I am of you.

Power is the ability and authority to recognize or reveal God. Revelation is God revealed, which is power. Response is God recognized, which again is power. So then:

Revelation = Power
Response = Power
Therefore
Power + Power = Powerful Power!

Do you want power? Get behind God, daughter. Get behind Jesus, wife. Get behind the Holy Spirit, vessel. Find your place of rest and stay there, through every trial, issue, habit or heartbreak. The only way through the wilderness is "*through* the wilderness." But you have the promise of powerful power with you, and that promise will keep you no matter how difficult it gets. When you understand the source and the location of your power through rest, you have found the source of your strength, joy and peace. You have unlocked the "the shelter of the most high" and found a place for yourself "under the shadow of the Almighty" (see Ps. 91:1).

I journeyed to Kearny, New Jersey, to spend some special time with my friend and sister in the Lord, Dr. Judy Brown. Her mom had just died. It was a difficult season, but I saw her strength. She was resting. She had found the underground river of her joy. She even found time away from her grief to give me a gift of her creativity that I'd like to share with you.

It's Inside You!
by
Dr. Judy Brown
(a.k.a. Susan Hurbs)

It's all inside you
The things that you seek!
Look in your heart
And in your soul...
You will see you are not weak!

You say but I am empty
There is nothing inside
Look again
I am sure you will want to abide.

In a little corner tucked away
Behind the hurt and pain
There is a surprise package with a lot to gain...
Such as love for yourself and others,
The forgiving person that you are
But isn't that what bothers?
No, not if I had my druthers
For inside you there is strength and
Power and it is increased to you hour by hour.
It is inside you
All the things you need to make
You strong as a tower!

There is nothing like the power that comes from a life surrendered to and led by the Spirit. Tribulation is a fact of life, but it's never a fact worth fearing when we're resting in the One who has overcome every tribulation we will ever face. Victory is ours if we choose to walk in it. A sovereign God decided that it would be so before He pulled us from our mothers' wombs. The outcome never has to come into question. The world may wonder how things are going to turn out, but we only look with wonder at an awesome God who already told us how everything ends... It doesn't.

Who are you, woman of power? You are His forever.

From My Heart

"The Right Response"

How do you respond when God reveals Himself to you in a circumstance? When faced with a revelation of truth that requires a godly, but difficult, response on our part, Scripture provides us with a number of examples to follow.

- **The Shunammite woman** (2 Kings 4:8-37): *"It is well."*
- **Mary** (Lk. 1:26-38): *"Be it unto me according to thy word."*
- **Isaiah** (Is. 6:1-8): *"Here am I; send me."*
- **Abraham** (Gen. 22:1-8): *"God will provide."*
- **David** (2 Sam. 6:14): *"David danced before the Lord with all his might."*
- **Job** (Job 1:21): *"The Lord gave, and the Lord hath taken away."*
- **Moses** (Ex. 14): *"Fear ye not, stand still, and see the salvation of the Lord."*
- **Jesus** (Lk. 22:39-46): *"Nevertheless not My will, but Thine, be done."*

Can you think of situations in your life where one or more of these responses were required? Choose one and write about it.

From Your Heart

Prayer for Power

"Search my heart, Father, and show me the things that do not please You. Show me my stubbornness and my pride. Expose my insecurity and any issue of trust. Shed light on everything that would hinder me from giving You my heart. Then, Lord, my desire is to know You as You are, not as I wish You to be or as others have explained You to me. Show me the way to intimacy with You as I have never known it. Give me a thirst for You and a longing for Your attention, Your presence and Your affection. Always be enough for me. Finally, Holy Spirit, fill me to overflowing with all You have to offer. I am a broken vessel, but I desire to be used by You, for God's glory. Teach me how to recognize the truth and ask for wisdom. Constrain me...control me...comfort me...care for me when I won't care for myself.

"God, I want to be available for You. Show me how to love You daily. I want to be a fit dwelling place for You, holy and acceptable. Purge me and prune me until You are satisfied, and when I complain, Lord, remind me of my desire to please You today. Lord, I present myself to You now. Amen."